TRANSLATIONS AND REPRINTS FROM THE
ORIGINAL SOURCES OF HISTORY
PUBLISHED BY THE DEPARTMENT OF HISTORY OF THE
UNIVERSITY OF PENNSYLVANIA

Third Series

Edited by
JOHN L. LAMONTE

Volume III

FEUDAL INSTITUTIONS

THE ASSIZES OF ROMANIA

UNIVERSITY OF PENNSYLVANIA

DEPARTMENT OF HISTORY

TRANSLATIONS AND REPRINTS FROM THE ORIGINAL SOURCES OF HISTORY

Edited by JOHN L. LAMONTE

First Series

Many issues still in print; details available on request.

Second Series

Volume 3. THE HISTORY OF THE LANGOBARDS BY PAUL THE DEACON. Translated by WILLIAM DUDLEY FOULKE.

Other volumes in this series are out of print.

Third Series

Volume 1. FULCHER OF CHARTRES: CHRONICLE OF THE FIRST CRUSADE. Translated by MARTHA EVELYN MCGINTY.

Volume 2. THE CAPTURE OF DAMIETTA BY OLIVER OF PADERBORN. Translated by JOHN J. GAVIGAN.

Volume 3. FEUDAL INSTITUTIONS: THE ASSIZES OF ROMANIA. Translated by PETER W. TOPPING.

Feudal Institutions

AS REVEALED IN THE

Assizes of Romania

THE LAW CODE OF FRANKISH GREECE

Translation of the Text of the Assizes
with a Commentary on Feudal Institutions
in Greece and in Medieval Europe

By

PETER W. TOPPING

ASSISTANT PROFESSOR OF HISTORY
UNIVERSITY OF CALIFORNIA: SANTA BARBARA COLLEGE

Philadelphia

UNIVERSITY OF PENNSYLVANIA PRESS

London: Geoffrey Cumberlege
Oxford University Press

1949

Manufactured in the United States of America

FOREWORD

The present volume differs from others in the *Translations and Reprints* in that it is not only a translation of an important medieval document, but also a general study of feudal institutions throughout medieval Europe with special reference to the Frankish crusader state of Morea. The Assizes of Romania are not the greatest code of feudal law extant but are a very representative compilation of feudal customs from the later Middle Ages, and are especially full on matters of private law. Further, they are short enough so that they can be translated in their entirety in a single small volume. In point of time the Assizes of Romania stand towards the end of the development of feudal custom law and thus make a most interesting comparison with the early Burgundian Code which will be published in this series.

In addition to translating the code, Dr. Topping has prepared a commentary on feudal law, which is published here as the second part of the volume. In this commentary he has taken up the chief points of feudal law and studied them in the various countries of medieval Europe, comparing the practices of Morea with those of other contemporary states. It is hoped that this commentary will prove a useful manual for the study of feudal institutions generally.

It has long been recognized that feudal institutions and law were preserved in a purer form in the crusader states than in the kingdoms of western Europe. In most of the western law codes, principles of Roman law or the influence of royal justice had crept into the laws before they were written down. Only in the east do we find written codes of what is essentially the earlier purer feudal law, and though our code may date from the fourteenth century, the law it reflects is that of a much earlier age, which had been perpetuated in the conservative environment of the crusader colonies. In this respect the Assizes of Romania are like the great books of John d'Ibelin and Philip de Novare in Jerusalem and Cyprus.

One characteristic of feudal law is especially well brought out in this code. Often the author will ask a question to which he gives several contradictory answers. Nothing illustrates more clearly than this the essentially customary character of feudal law. It was never a matter of statute or of codified legislation; it was always the custom of the country as remembered by the men versed in the law. Law was never made, always found, and in Morea at least, divergent answers were occasionally found in the memories of different authorities. In his commentary, Dr. Topping has endeavored to answer some of these questions through a comparative study of the laws of other countries, and if he has so steeped himself in the Assizes that he follows the author in his habit of asking rhetorical questions, it is to be hoped that his answers will be found equally satisfactory, if not more so.

Several issues of the first series of the *Translations and Reprints* were devoted to documents illustrating feudalism. In publishing this complete code of feudal law and the commentary thereon, the editor feels that this tradition is being carried on with a significant contribution to the sources of feudal institutions available in English translation.

JOHN L. LAMONTE

PREFACE

This volume is a revision of a doctoral dissertation submitted at the University of Pennsylvania in 1942, but, so far as the commentary on feudal institutions is concerned, completely reorganized and rewritten as a result of further study both in this country and in Europe.[1] To Professor John L. LaMonte of the University of Pennsylvania, at whose suggestion the work was originally undertaken, I am indebted for encouragement and guidance both in the preparation of the original dissertation and in revising it for inclusion in this series, of which he is the editor.

I have in addition benefited from the valuable suggestions made to me by Professor Henri Grégoire, Vice-President of the Institut de Philologie et d'Histoire Orientales et Slaves of the University of Brussels, and M. Jean Longnon, Conservateur-adjoint of the Library of the Institut de France. My long discussions with these distinguished savants are a cherished memory and were made possible by the generosity of the Belgian American Educational Foundation, which made me the recipient of an advanced Fellowship. To the officers of this Foundation, as well as to those of the Social Science Research Council, who saw fit to award me a supplementary grant, I wish to express my gratitude for the opportunity to study abroad in the period January, 1947–August, 1948.

Whatever merit and interest this study may possess are due to the teachers and friends I have named. Its shortcomings are entirely my own.

I wish also to thank Dr. Mary Elizabeth Nickerson and my brother Nicholas for their valuable assistance, especially in preparing the manuscript for the printers.

Peter W. Topping

Santa Barbara, California

[1] A microfilm copy of the original dissertation is on deposit in the Library of the University of Pennsylvania. In the original, the discussion of feudal institutions is given in the form of a commentary on the individual chapters of the text of the Assizes.

CONTENTS

Map

FRANKISH GREECE
XIII Century
MILES
KILOMETERS
Durazzo
PELAGONIA
Salonika
EPIRUS
CORFU
VLACHIA
Larissa
Ravennika
NEGROPONT
Neopatras
Boudonitza
(Thermopylae)
Lepanto
Thebes
CEPHALONIA
Glarentza
Patras
Chalandritsa
Chloumoutsi
Kalavryta
Corinth
Athens
EUBOEA
ZANTE
(ZAKYNTHOS)
Andravida
Akova
(Matagriffon)
Argos
Beauvoir
Karytaina
ARCHIPELAGO
Androusa
Lacedaemonia
Kalamata
Mistra
Navarino
NAXOS
Beaufort
Passavant
Monemvasia
Old Maïna
ROMANIE
ATHENS
MOREA
ANJOU
Candia
CRETE

INTRODUCTION

THE PRINCIPALITY OF MOREA

Modern historians, while recognizing the great importance of the religious impulse in inaugurating and sustaining the Crusades, have also come to view them as large-scale attempts at feudal colonization and commercial expansion. A classic illustration for the second interpretation is the Fourth Crusade of 1199 to 1204. That it took place during the pontificate of the strongest of the medieval popes, Innocent III, is an ironical reminder of the extent to which the Crusades had by 1200 become a largely lay movement directed to secular ends. A leading participant in the Fourth Crusade, Geoffrey de Villehardouin, Marshal of Champagne, in his graphic narrative which is one of the earliest monuments of French historical prose—a "giant lisping" someone has called it—has told the traditional story of the enterprise. He relates how the Crusaders contracted with Venice for transportation to Egypt; how, when they were unable to pay for this service, they accepted the Republic's suggestion that they assist her in capturing the Christian port of Zara on the Dalmatian coast; and how, finally, Venetians and Crusaders together seized the opportunity afforded by a dynastic struggle to divert the expedition to the capture of Constantinople and the overthrow of the Byzantine Empire.[1]

The whole astonishing adventure, crowned with bewildering

[1] Acceptance or rejection of Villehardouin's account is the main basis on which have been founded the "theory of accidents" and the "theory of premeditation" to explain the diversion of the Fourth Crusade. Opinion of recent investigators like A. A. Vasiliev, J. Bédier, and Edmond Faral has veered toward the "theory of accidents." However, in the latest treatment of the question, Henri Grégoire vigorously insists that Boniface of Montferrat entertained the plan of conquering Constantinople from the time he was elected commander of the crusading host ("The Question of the Diversion of the Fourth Crusade, or, An Old Controversy Solved by a Latin Adverb," *Byzantion,* vol. XV [1940–41], pp. 158–66).

success, was a political revolution of incalculable effect in the subsequent history of the Near East. In its immediate results it led to the establishment of the Venetian colonial empire and a number of crusading states within the former limits of the Byzantine Empire. The most important of these states were the Latin Empire of Constantinople, the Kingdom of Salonika, the Principality of Achaia or Morea, the Lordship (later Duchy) of Athens, and the Duchy of the Archipelago. Despite their greater extent and prestige, the Latin Empire and the Kingdom of Salonika were destined to have but a short and precarious existence. The former enjoyed a brief period of glory and imperial influence under Henry of Flanders (1206–16); after his premature death it had little political importance and disappeared completely with the Greek recapture of Constantinople in 1261. The Kingdom of Salonika had an even more ephemeral existence, disappearing in 1224 upon the conquest of its capital city by the Greek Despot of Epirus, Theodore Angelus. On the other hand, the states of Achaia and Athens lasted for over two centuries, and the Duchy of the Archipelago for more than three and a half. Of these by far the strongest in the thirteenth century and the most interesting from the point of view of feudal institutions was the Principality of Achaia. It is of this crusading state that the "Book of the Customs of the Empire of Romania"—which is presented in translation below, and which we shall more conveniently refer to as the "Assizes of Romania"—was the code of feudal usages and customs.[2]

The Principality of Achaia or Morea,[3] which in geographical extent was almost exactly synonymous with the classical peninsula of Peloponnesus, was established through the efforts of two French knights: Guillaume de Champlitte, who hailed from Franche-

[2] The fuller title is the translation of the Latin *Liber de consuetudinibus Imperii Romanie*. "Romania" designated the East Roman, or Byzantine, Empire, and after 1204 was applied to the Latin Empire of Constantinople and the Frankish states nominally subject to it. The Assizes of Romania, however, despite their title, were essentially a feudal code of the Principality of Achaia. (On the use of the term "Romania" see especially Robert Lee Wolff, "Romania: the Latin Empire of Constantinople," *Speculum*, XXIII [1948], pp. 1–34.)

[3] Achaia in ancient times was the district on the northern coast of Peloponnesus; it became the provincial name of the greater part of Greece under the Roman Emperors. Morea was the name most often applied to Peloponnesus in the late medieval and Turkish periods.

Comté, and Geoffrey de Villehardouin of Champagne, a nephew of the chronicler. With a handful of knights they rapidly conquered most of the peninsula in 1205 so that by November of that year Innocent III was able to refer to Champlitte in a letter as "Prince of all Achaia." After Champlitte's death Villehardouin obtained the principality through a piece of chicanery when he managed, as bailie of Achaia, to avoid seeing the lawful heir, just arrived from France, within a year and a day, the period agreed upon for making the claim to the principality (1210). However, in this case the end seemed to justify the means, for Geoffrey had been the real author of the conquest of Morea and proved himself an able ruler respected alike by the proud barons of the Conquest and by the native Greek population. He completed the feudal organization of the peninsula begun by Champlitte and did homage to Emperor Henry, receiving the office of Seneschal of Romania. He also came to terms with Venice over the Republic's strategic and commercial interests in Morea, and further consolidated his rule by reducing three of the four strongholds remaining in Greek hands. In 1217 he arranged the marriage of his elder son and heir, Geoffrey, to Agnes, daughter of the Latin Emperor Peter of Courtenay.[4]

Geoffrey II (ca. 1228–1246) continued the wise and able rule of his father and was regarded as the strongest prince in the "New France" created on the ruins of Byzantium. In 1236, after lending decisive aid to the defense of Constantinople against Greek and Bulgarian attacks, he received from Emperor Baldwin II the suzerainty over the island of Negropont (the classical Euboea), the Marquisate of Boudonitza (the marcher state guarding Thermopylae), and possibly over the Duchy of the Archipelago. An even more striking testimonial to his strength as a feudal ruler was the voluntary submission to him as overlord by the Despot Manuel of Epirus and the Count of Cephalonia and Zante.[5]

[4] Geoffrey seems still to have been alive in 1228; certainly it was he, rather than his son Geoffrey, who was involved in the bitter struggle with the Latin clergy of Morea and Pope Honorius III from 1219 to 1223. (On the corrected chronology see Jean Longnon, "Problèmes de l'histoire de la principauté de Morée. Deuxième article," *Journal des Savants*, July–Dec., 1946, pp. 157 ff.)

[5] The rulers of all of these vassal states, with the exception of the Despot of Epirus, were among the peers of the prince at the time the Assizes of Romania were written down in the early fourteenth century (see article 43). The Archi-

William de Villehardouin, the brother and successor of Geoffrey II, during his long rule from 1246 to 1278 played an even more prominent role in the affairs of his time. He brought the Frankish sway in Achaia to its zenith when he forced the surrender of the last Greek stronghold of the peninsula, Monemvasia, the "Gibraltar of Greece," and constructed three castles in the south—the famous Mistrâ, Old Maina, and Beaufort—to reduce unruly tribes in that area to submission. In the three-year siege of Monemvasia he used his position as a powerful suzerain to good advantage, receiving substantial aid from the important vassals of the principality—the "Great Lord" of Athens, the rulers of Negropont, the Duke of the Archipelago, and the Count of Cephalonia. William reached the height of his prestige in Frankish affairs when he defeated a coalition of barons headed by Guy de la Roche, "Great Lord" of Athens, which sought to prevent him from inheriting the northern third of Negropont, of which his deceased second wife had been baroness in her own right.[6]

The history of Frankish Greece is characterized by some remarkable reversals of fortune, and one of the most sudden and dramatic was the capture and complete humiliation of William by the Greeks of Nicaea only a year after his triumph over Athens and Negropont. Again, conjugal interests involved him in an important struggle. For he had taken as his third wife Anna, a daughter of the Despot Michael II of Epirus, and he readily answered his father-in-law's appeal for aid in the impending contest between Epirus and the Empire of Nicaea for supremacy in the Greek world. We may

---

pelago was certainly a vassal state of Morea under Prince William and again in the fourteenth century. On the question of Baldwin's granting suzerainty to Geoffrey II see Longnon, *ibid.*, pp. 149 ff.

[6] An interesting consequence of this conflict—if the Chronicle of Morea is to be believed—was the conferring of the title of duke on the defeated ruler of Athens by Louis IX of France, to whose court Guy had been sent to stand trial for having taken up arms against his liege lord, William. The anachronistic use of the title of Duke of Athens in literature by Dante, Boccaccio, Chaucer, and Shakespeare is thus due to the fact that medieval Athens was for two centuries ruled by dukes, who were successively Frenchmen, Aragonese, and Florentines. (Jean Longnon has recently shown that it was rather the brother of St. Louis, Charles I d'Anjou, or the latter's son, who conferred the title of duke on the lords of Athens in the 1280's. "Problèmes de l'histoire de la principauté de Morée," *Journal des Savants*, April–June, 1946, pp. 90–91.)

readily speculate that the ambitious prince, so typically feudal in his love of fighting and desire for aggrandizement, entertained notions of expanding his realm and suzerainty into central and northern Greece. The contending sides met on the plain of Pelagonia in Western Macedonia (October 1259), and when the Epirote armies deserted, the prince and his splendid Achaian chivalry, with other Frankish contingents, were left alone to face the imperial forces, and they went down in disastrous defeat. William was taken prisoner and was released in 1262 only on the harsh condition that he surrender the three castles of Mistrâ, Monemvasia, and Old Maina to the Byzantine Emperor, Michael VIII Palaiologos, the victor of Pelagonia, who in 1261 had transferred his seat of empire from Nicaea to Constantinople.

When the captured Prince was first taken before the Emperor, the Greek ruler offered him a large sum of money if he would cede the entire principality and return to the country of his ancestors to purchase lands and settle down there. The Prince's reply, as recorded in the *Chronicle of Morea,* is remarkable as a cogent statement of feudal principles. After rejecting Michael's offer as impossible of acceptance, even were the Emperor to hold him in prison "for five-and-fifty years," the prince continued:

For I do not, Sire, hold that land of Morea either as a paternal or ancestral inheritance, so that I can freely give and grant it away. Those well-born men conquered the land who came with my father from France hither to Romania, as his friends and companions-in-arms. By the sword did they gain the land of Morea, and among themselves they made just distribution of it. To each they gave according to his quality, and thereafter they all chose and made my father, as the man of greatest honor and wisdom among them, leader over all. They set down in written agreements and conventions that he should have no power to make judgment alone, nor indeed to do anything in the world, without the counsel and will of all his companions. And thus, Sire, I am without power to give up anything of the land that I hold, because our fathers gained it by the sword, according to the customs that we hold and that they made in common.[7]

[7] Lines 4271–4290 of the Greek version of the *Chronicle of Morea,* John Schmitt, ed., (London, 1904). Compare the statement of Balian of Sidon to the bailies of Frederick II in 1231 (*Le Livre d'Eracles,* in: *Recueil des Historiens des Croisades, Historiens Occidentaux,* II, 389).

In conclusion William declared that the Emperor, as was the feudal custom, could exact a ransom from each captive according to his substance, and each one would exert himself to his utmost to purchase his release.

The Emperor conveniently ignored feudal custom and kept the French nobles in prison for three years until William agreed to cede the three powerful fortresses in the southeastern corner of Morea. In the principality itself the High Court met in a memorable session—a "parliament of dames" consisting of the widows and wives of the knights slain or captured at Pelagonia—to approve the cession of the castles. Duke Guy of Athens opposed the cession, pointing out that the reintroduction of Byzantine rule in Morea would be fatal to the Frankish principality, and arguing that it were better that the Prince should perish in prison than that the rest of the Franks should lose their patrimony. But the strength of conjugal sentiment overcame Guy's plea to save the state.

The bitter warfare that quickly broke out between Franks and Greeks in Morea became in a few years an important part of the wider conflict between Charles of Anjou and the Byzantine Empire. As the new ruler of Naples and Sicily, Charles inherited the expansionist Eastern policy of his Norman and Hohenstaufen predecessors—a medieval *Drang nach Osten*. He obtained more than a strong legal basis for his ambitious design in the form of two treaties which he concluded in the Pope's residence at Viterbo in May 1267, with William de Villehardouin and Baldwin II, the refugee Latin Emperor. In the first (May 24) the Prince of Achaia—so desirous was he to obtain the aid and protection of the powerful French ruler, now his close neighbor—ceded the principality to the House of Anjou, with the understanding that he would hold it for the rest of his life as vassal prince of the Angevins and that his daughter and heir would marry one of Charles's sons.[8] By the

[8] As a result Isabelle, William's daughter, married Philip, the second son of Charles. Philip died in 1277 before his father-in-law, and the title reverted to his father Charles at the death of William. William was severely restricted in the infeudations he could make which would be valid after his death; and any fiefs he might create in a port town or castle could be revoked by his successors. (Jean Longnon, "Le Rattachement de la Principauté de Morée au royaume de Sicile en 1267," *Journal des Savants,* July–Sept., 1942, p. 136, where the provisions of the treaty of May 24 are given for the first time, on the basis of a recently discovered manuscript.)

second treaty of Viterbo (May 27) Baldwin II transferred to Charles most of his rights to the Latin Empire and its vassal states, including the suzerainty over Morea. William and a large contingent of the famous knights of Morea distinguished themselves in Charles's campaign against the last Hohenstaufen claimant, and in return the Prince received substantial aid from his suzerain in the warfare with the Greeks of Mistrâ. But as events were soon to show, the Angevin connection was mainly a source of woes for the Frankish states of Greece. When William died in 1278, Charles I, now both prince and suzerain of Morea, inaugurated an intermittent absentee rule through unpopular bailiffs unable to win the respect of the proud and unruly native Frankish barons; at other times dynastic intrigues and disputed successions marked by disastrous civil conflict harassed the principality. For brief periods, like the joint rule in residence of Isabelle de Villehardouin and her second husband, Florent d'Avesnes of Hainault (1289–97), Frankish Morea experienced a return of its prosperity and influence under the first three Villehardouins.[9] After Florent's untimely death Isabelle married again and once more ruled Frankish Morea in residence, with her third husband, Philip of Savoy (1301–07). But Philip chose to regard Achaia as a land to be exploited for purely personal profit, and his policy of systematic extortion, together with his refusal to serve his Neapolitan suzerain in war, led the latter to deprive him and Isabelle of their princedom. The luckless daughter of the last Villehardouin prince died in Holland in 1311, far from the classic land that her adventurous grandfather and his companions had conquered. She had stoically endured the fate of having to submit to three purely political marriages required by the conscienceless Eastern policy of the Angevin kings. That policy had never succeeded in its grandiose aim of conquering the Greek Empire, and in 1377 the Angevins finally wearied of the reduced principality of Morea to the point of pawning it for five years to the Knights of the Hospital of St. John of Jerusalem. The Hospital was in turn succeeded by a body of military adven-

[9] Isabelle, elder daughter of William, in 1289 received her father's state as a fief from Charles II of Anjou (who made the grant out of "pure liberality and special grace"), upon the recommendation of the Moreot barons, who pointed out the advantages of rule by a resident prince married to the Villehardouin heiress.

turers from Navarre. The last Prince of Achaia, a baron of Genoese origin, in 1430 surrendered to the Byzantine Greeks the remnant of the Frankish state, but the Greeks were within another generation to lose the entire peninsula to the all-conquering Ottoman Turks.

The heroic age of the Principality of Achaia was the first and predominantly French century of its existence. The stable and virile state which the Villehardouin princes organized in a conquered country with a civilization far older than that of Western Europe is striking proof of the practicality and adaptability of the feudal system of political and social organization. For several reasons, especially the schism between Greek and Latin Catholicism, no fusion of Franks and Greeks occurred; nevertheless a rather high degree of coöperation and mutual toleration of races was achieved under the wise rule of the male Villehardouins, which was an undoubted improvement over the Byzantine administration on the eve of the Frankish conquest. The exploitation of "colonial" Morea by the expanding French feudalism of the thirteenth century was not as naked or abusive as that by Philip of Savoy or the Florentine banking house of the Acciajuoli in the fourteenth century. Of Geoffrey II Villehardouin we read in a reliable Venetian source that:

> He possessed a broad domain and great riches; he was wont to send his most confidential advisers from time to time to the courts of his vassals, to see how they lived and how they treated their subjects. At his own court he constantly maintained eighty knights with golden spurs, to whom he gave all that they required besides their pay; so knights came from France, from Burgundy, and, above all, from Champagne, to follow him. Some came to amuse themselves, others to pay their debts, others because of crimes which they had committed at home.[10]

In William's time, the same source relates, "there was in the principality so much politeness and goodness that not alone the knights but also the merchants traveled up and down [the peninsula]

[10] Marino Sanudo Torsello, "Istoria del Regno di Romania," in C. Hopf, *Chroniques gréco-romanes inédites ou peu connues* (Berlin, 1873), pp. 100–1; translation quoted from Wm. Miller, *The Latins in the Levant* (London, 1908), p. 87.

without money and lodged in the house of the bailies and with their simple note of hand obtained money and paid their expenses abundantly." Such was the magnificence of William's court that it appeared larger than the court of a great king. Seven hundred to one thousand knights were in constant attendance upon the Prince, and when William went to meet Saint Louis in Cyprus on his crusade he made the passage with about twenty-four "galleys and vessels" and four hundred "good knights." [11]

THE CHRONICLE OF MOREA

A fuller and more vivid picture of the society and activity of the Villehardouin princes emerges from the Chronicle of Morea, a lengthy narrative work which has come down to us in four versions in as many languages [12] and in its original form was composed early in the fourteenth century. Its central subject and hero is William de Villehardouin, and it succeeds in conveying the spirit alike of the adventurous and warlike barons of the Conquest and of the reigns of the vigorous Villehardouin princes. "It supplies the local colour, the personal touch, and the sense of realistic environment, without which the story of the Frankish princes of Achaia . . . would remain somewhat barren of interest." [13]

From the Chronicle we learn of the division of the country into fiefs at the Conquest, of the creation of twelve great baronies whose holders with the other lieges formed a High Court to advise the Prince and decide legal questions, of the creation of ecclesiastical baronies, of the establishment of the three great military-religious orders of the Templars, Hospitallers, and Teutonic

[11] Sanudo in Hopf, *Chroniques gréco-romanes*, pp. 101–2, 151–52. There is good reason for regarding William as the author of two troubadour songs in the important collection known as "Le Manuscrit du Roi," whose first owner was Charles d'Anjou. (See Jean Longnon, "Le Prince de Morée Chansonnier," *Romania*, LXV (1939), 95–100.)

[12] Greek, French, Aragonese, and Italian (see Bibliography for editions). On the complicated question of the origin of the Chronicle and the relationship of the versions to one another see A. I. Adamantiou, "Ta Chronika tou Moreos" (in Modern Greek), in *Deltion tes Historikes kai Ethnologikes Hetaireias tes Hellados*, VI (Athens, 1906), pp. 453–675, and the Introduction to Jean Longnon's edition of the French version.

[13] Sir Rennell Rodd, *The Princes of Achaia and the Chronicles of Morea: a Study of Greece in the Middle Ages* (2 vols., London, 1907), I, 4.

Knights, of the existence of Grand Officers, and of numerous other arrangements. The military service required of the various categories of fief-holders is exactly specified, and the Chronicle here accords with the Assizes of Romania in leaving the impression that military service, with a few exceptions, was required practically the year around. The Franks were a mere handful of invaders in the midst of a native population overwhelmingly superior in numbers. They instinctively appreciated the value of the remarkable strategic positions that Peloponnesus possesses, and the impressive ruins of some of the castles which they built at these points still dominate the surrounding countryside. One great castle and barony in Arcadia bore the significant name of Matagrifon, meaning "Kill-Greek" or "Stop-Greek."

There is much more that the Chronicle of Morea tells us—of noble acts and knightly adventures, of lengthy feudal cases and successful or disastrous campaigns, and of a brilliant tournament that was held on the isthmus of Corinth and lasted for twenty days; to it came the entire chivalry of Frankish Greece and even some challengers from beyond the seas—*d'outre mer,*—eager to test their skill against the highly reputed chivalry of "New France." The Chronicle, unlike many works of its genre, is no dry narrative of events. It is in fact akin to the *chansons de geste* in the way it combines elements of history and legend and seeks to inspire its readers or listeners by recalling to them the *gestes* of the brave warriors of the Conquest and of those who came after them, especially during the reign of the warlike Prince William. From internal evidence it seems highly probable that the work was written to be read or recited in public; indeed, the Greek Chronicle, unlike the other three versions, is written in verse, in the most common meter of vernacular medieval and modern Greek poetry. Although the Chronicle of Morea is not a first-rate source for political and military history, it remains a very valuable institutional and sociological source because of its faithful and accurate depiction of local and feudal customs, even of folk legends and superstitions, and above all of the workings of legal processes in the feudal courts of Morea. The lengthy recital of the great cases that came before the High Court is so detailed and technically accurate that it is reasonable to suppose that the writer copied contemporary records, perhaps the very minutes of the cases.

As a literary work the Chronicle is undistinguished, yet this curious production of the hybrid Frankish-Greek society is the indirect inspiration of an episode in one of the world's literary masterpieces. In the third act of the second part of *Faust*, Goethe by a daring fancy depicts the mystic union of German romanticism and Greek classicism as personified by Faust and Helena. The scene is partly laid in "a fortress inaccessible," which is the Mistrâ of the Chronicle and which is identified with ancient Sparta. Faust is the feudal lord of the fortress; as such he can be satisfactorily identified with one of the Villehardouin princes and especially with William, and his consort with William's third wife, the Greek princess Anna of Epirus.[14]

THE ASSIZES OF ROMANIA

To complete and supplement the picture of feudal Morea which the Chronicle presents, to learn more comprehensively the various workings of Moreot feudalism in terms of the mutual obligations and services of lord and vassal, of homage and investiture, of justice and wardship, of the granting and disposition of lands, we must turn to the formal code of customs and usages of Achaia—to the so-called Assizes of Romania themselves. They have reached us as a code of 219 articles which derive from a recording made in the early fourteenth century, very probably under Angevin auspices. This recording in turn probably rested, at least in part, on a

[14] Cf. G. Moravcsik, "Zur Quellenfrage der Helenaepisode in Goethes Faust," *Byzantinisch-neugriechische Jahrbücher*, VIII (1929–30; published in Athens, 1931), pp. 41–56. In the years immediately preceding 1825, when he gave to the "Helena episode" its final form, Goethe had read widely on the topography of Morea, and on the Fourth Crusade and the establishment of feudalism in Greece. While he did not know the Chronicle of Morea directly, Moravcsik has plausibly demonstrated that he must have known the later chronicle (also in vernacular Greek) of Dorotheos of Monemvasia, which uses the Greek Chronicle of Morea as the chief source for its account of Frankish Morea, and which not only identifies Mistrâ with Sparta but expressly calls Princess Anna a "second Helen of Menelaus." (Mistrâ is actually on a spur of the famous Taygetus range a few miles from the ancient and modern towns of Sparta on the plain below. It is a very strong position which the ancient Spartans had inexplicably overlooked.)

less complete code of the thirteenth century, consisting of records of various judgments of the High Court and of formulations of existing custom.[15] In any case the code we possess mirrors the feudal society of the conquerors of Morea and of the two or three succeeding generations. On numerous points it reflects the double circumstance of the conquest of Morea by a handful of barons led by one of their own number and class who was strictly *primus inter pares*, and of the necessity of frequent warfare and constant vigilance to defend and extend the country. Thus the barons of the Conquest and their descendants, together with the other liege lords, formed a privileged political and social class sharply set apart from the vassals of simple homage. Further, as we have already seen, military service was virtually a continuous requirement in all seasons, and on one notable occasion Geoffrey I drastically enforced the military service required of the ecclesiastical fiefs. These and other features of the Assizes of Romania make them significant for the general study of feudal institutions. Especially is this true in the realm of private law. They reflect, for example, a remarkable development of the community of goods between spouses; precariousness and revocability seem to distinguish several types of grants; there is an unusual treatment of the subject of investiture and seizin; the treatment of wardship—conjugal as well as that of minors—is rather detailed; and the miscellaneous provisions relating to procedure and justice suggest a vigorous development of baronial jurisdictions. The existence of a class of native Greek feudatories with some non-feudal traits, such as the custom of equal succession, lends further interest to the Assizes. Finally, they devote considerable space to the condition of the Moreot serfs, whose unfortunate lot was much the same as that of the mass of agricultural laborers in Western Europe.

While the Assizes are not very detailed or lengthy, they are comprehensive in scope and succeed in dealing with most of the important feudal processes and relationships. They are obviously not the work of a highly trained practitioner and master of the law. The author at times forgets the premises of an argument and displays a remarkable incapacity for abstraction and generaliza-

[15] Consult Peter W. Topping, "The Formation of the Assizes of Romania," *Byzantion*, XVII (1944–45), pp. 304–14.

tion. He can cite only specific questions at issue, he is repetitious and on occasion obscure, and he lacks any intelligent order in his exposition. But he is not dogmatic and will readily state two points of view on a controversial topic; he will sometimes ask questions that he leaves unanswered, and may even register a mild objection to a usage he has just stated. He lacks sophistication and displays little of the subtlety of the great masters of Jerusalemite jurisprudence, Philip de Novare and John d'Ibelin. But he has left us an honest recording of the law he knew, and it is this record of northern French law of the early thirteenth century as implanted and preserved in conquered Morea that justifies our viewing the Assizes of Romania as a "typical" code which reflects a good deal of western feudal practice before it has been changed under the influence of the growing royal administration and of the ideas of Roman law.

THE PRINCES OF MOREA, 1205–1383

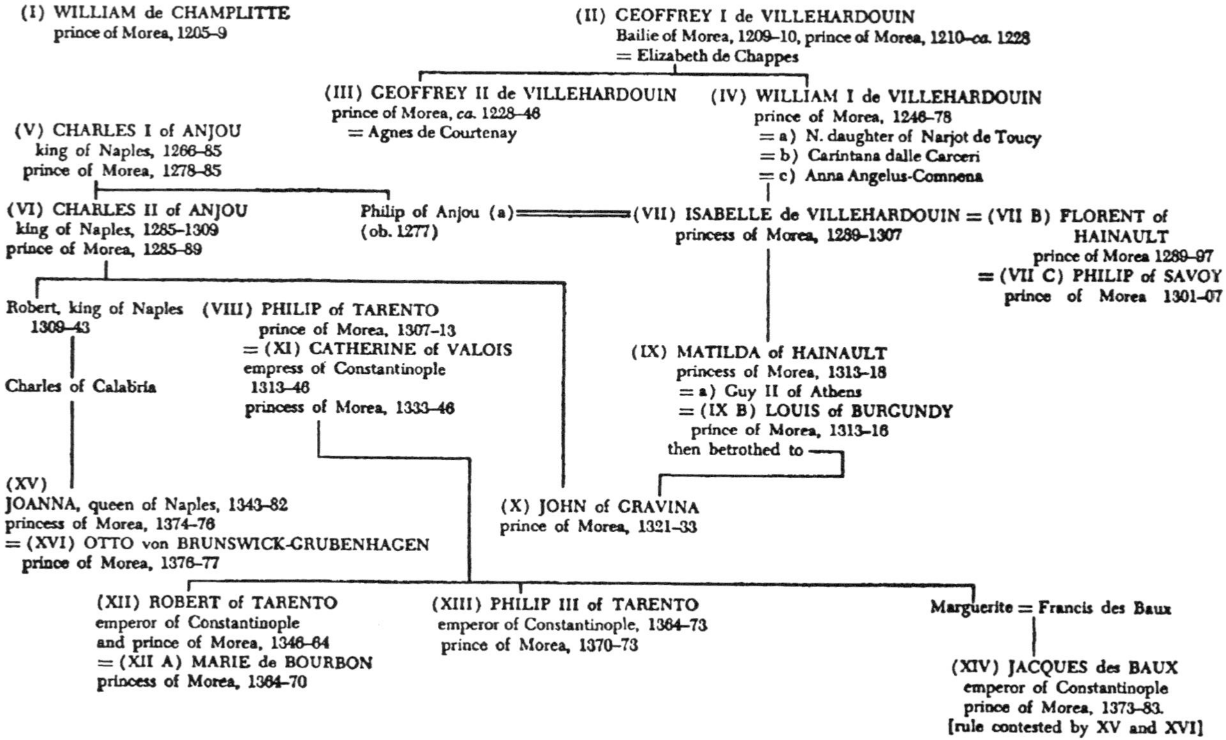

THE ASSIZES OF ROMANIA

THIS IS THE BOOK OF THE USAGES AND STATUTES OF THE EMPIRE OF ROMANIA, WHICH WERE ORDERED AND ESTABLISHED IN THE TIME OF THE MOST SERENE LORDS COUNT BALDWIN OF FLANDERS, SIRE BONIFACE, MARQUIS OF MONTFERRAT, SIRE HENRY DANDOLO, DOGE OF VENICE, AND MANY OTHER BARONS, AT THE TIME WHEN THE EMPIRE OF ROMANIA AND OF CONSTANTINOPLE WAS CONQUERED.

Prologue [1]

I

When the holy city of Jerusalem was conquered by the Christians and by the faith of Christ, and by the exhortation and preaching of Peter the Hermit, in the year of the incarnation of our Lord Jesus Christ 1104 [1099], the princes and the barons who had conquered it chose as King of the said Realm of Jerusalem Duke Godfrey of Bouillon. And when he received the lordship, he did not wish to be consecrated or named King of the said Realm, nor further did he wish to wear the crown of gold, there where the King of Kings, the Son of God, our Lord Jesus Christ, had worn the crown of thorns on the day of His Holy Passion; at first he desired to be crowned with a crown of straw. And thus the said Duke Godfrey, wishing to put the said Realm into such good state and good condition that all manner of men going and coming and remaining in the said Realm should be governed and protected and maintained by justice, right, and reason, took counsel with the patriarch of the said city of Jerusalem and with the other barons, princes, lords, and wise men who were there from various lands and divers countries; and having asked of each of them the usages and customs of his province and country, he ordered put into writing everything that each one said and that could be well understood. And then in his own presence and before his lordship the patriarch and all of the other princes and barons who took part in the said conquest he caused the document to be read and examined; and

[1] Part I of the Prologue is interpolated from John d'Ibelin's treatise on the laws of Jerusalem-Cyprus, part of the larger collection generally called *Assises de Jérusalem.* Cf. art. 3.

Throughout our translation we use "vassal" in two meanings, both of which should be clear from the context: 1) generically, in the sense of a feudatory or feudal tenant, that is, any member of the feudal hierarchy or class of fief-holding nobility; and 2) more narrowly, in the sense of a feudatory holding a fief from a particular lord, to whom he has vowed homage and fealty.

with the counsel of all it was made and constituted the usages and assizes which were to be maintained and held and kept in the said Realm of Jerusalem. Then Duke Godfrey established in the said Realm two secular courts: one was called the High Court and the other the Low Court, that is, the Court of the Bourgeois, to which he appointed a man to be governor and justiciar in his place who was called Viscount. And he appointed as judges of the High Court his barons and knights and vassals, whom he held enfeoffed to himself through the homage or oath which they had made. And to the Low Court, that is, that of the Bourgeois, he summoned the most loyal and the wisest burgesses whom he could find in the city, and had them swear the oath of the bourgeoisie as is provided in the Great Book of the Court of the Bourgeois. And the said king ordained that the knights and vassals be brought into and judged by the High Court while the other people, whom he did not wish to be taken into the High Court, be brought into and judged by the Court of the Bourgeois. And this was accomplished by the common accord of the lord and his barons. And after the said usages and assizes had been established, as was said above, they were mentioned and many times were amended by the other kings and lords who succeeded in the said Realm; for those things which they saw and recognized to be good they added thereto.

II

How, After the Conquest of Jerusalem [Constantinople] by the Above-mentioned Lords, They Sent to the King of Jerusalem and to the Patriarch to Ask Them to Send Their Usages, Knowing That It Was Desirable to Be Ruled by Them Since These Were Usages of Conquest.

And after the conquest of the holy city of Jerusalem [Constantinople] in the year of the incarnation of our Lord Jesus Christ 1197 [1204], when Count Baldwin of Flanders, Sire Boniface, Marquis of Montferrat, Sire Henry Dandolo, Doge of Venice, and the other barons and princes of France conquered the city of Constantinople, they elected as emperor and lord of the Empire of Constantinople and of Romania Count Baldwin of Flanders. And since he wished to put the said Empire of Romania in such good state and good condition that his men and people and all manner of folk going and coming in the said Empire should be governed and ordered by justice, right and reason; and since the city of Constantinople is surrounded by many kinds of people, and especially by people who do not obey the laws of Rome or by the other people who came on the said conquest; and since they could not rule the said Empire well except with the usages and assizes which exist in the lands of the West [East], it was agreed to send to Jerusalem to the king and the patriarch, asking them to send their usages and assizes, for they wished to be ruled by them since they were usages of conquest. And thus were these sent, and afterward they were read before all the barons, and it was ordained that they be ruled by the said method and by the articles which should be most necessary for the said country of Romania. And it was thus ordered and sworn throughout all the Empire to hold and maintain and preserve the said usages, each according to his own power.

III

How, After the Death of the Emperor Baldwin, Sire Robert of Flanders, His Brother, Was Made Emperor, and How Sire Geoffrey de Villehardouin Took as His Wife the Daughter of Sire Robert.

And after the death of the Emperor Baldwin, Sire Robert of Flanders, his brother, was made Emperor, and he had a son and a daughter, and his son was named Baldwin and after the death of his father was Emperor for a long time, but then he lost the empire and went to the West, as is clearly told in the Book of Conquest.[1] At this time, the said Sire Robert, the Emperor, sent one of his daughters to the King of Aragon, and as the galleys were transporting the said lady, they came to the castle of Beauvoir, and Sire Geoffrey de Villehardouin, the elder brother of Prince William, who was called Lord of Morea, wishing to do honor to the daughter of the Emperor, so arranged that the lady descended from the galleys to the land. And since the said Sire Geoffrey had no wife, on the counsel of his barons he married the said lady; and from

[1] This account is of course quite wrong: see the following note for the correct narrative of events.

this sprang many wars and many scandals between the said Sire Robert, the Emperor, and the said Geoffrey de Villehardouin. And afterward, the said Sire Geoffrey, so wise was he and so persuasive, in the year of the incarnation of our Lord Jesus Christ one thousand and . . . [1209], in the month of May, being present with the Emperor Robert in the city of Larissa in Vlachia, came to an agreement with him whereby, according to the peace made between the two, the Emperor Robert granted to the said Sire Geoffrey de Villehardouin the isles of Romania that are called the Archipelago and made him Grand Seneschal of the Empire of Romania with the title of Prince of Achaia. And he ordered that the Prince was to hold the Principality of the Emperor. And he thus did homage to the Emperor. And then he ordained and swore to keep and to maintain the Usages and Customs of the Empire of Romania throughout the country in the manner written and set forth in this book.[2]

[2] The foregoing account of the derivation of the Assizes of Romania—which were really the code of Achaia—from a code of the Latin Empire which in turn was borrowed from Jerusalem has rightly been regarded as highly suspect. The author of the Assizes seems deliberately to be giving to his compilation the prestige of a Jerusalemite connection. At the end of the second part of the prologue we are told that those articles or chapters of the law of Jerusalem were borrowed that were "most necessary" for Romania. If so we might expect to find a close correspondence between many articles of the Assizes and parts of the *Assises de Jérusalem,* but this is not the case. (On this entire problem see P. W. Topping, "The Formation of the Assizes of Romania," *Byzantion,* XVII (1944–45), 304–14. For an interpretation closer to the Prologue's account, see J. L. LaMonte, "Three Questions Concerning the *Assises de Jérusalem,*" *Byzantina-Metabyzantina,* I (New York, 1946), part I, 201–11.)

The story told in Part III is badly confused, especially in genealogy, and may be corrected as follows: The first Latin Emperor, Baldwin, fell into the hands of the Bulgarians in 1205, disappearing from history, and was succeeded by his brother Henry (1206–16), the ablest of his line and the real founder of the Empire. Upon Henry's death their brother-in-law, Peter de Courtenay, Count of Auxerre and husband of their sister Yolande, was chosen Emperor by the barons of Constantinople to reign with his wife, but he was fated never to reach his empire. After being crowned by Pope Honorius III in 1217 on his way East, Peter crossed over from Brindisi to Durazzo and intended to march overland to his capital. But he was captured by the troops of the Despot of Epirus and died in prison, perhaps unnaturally. The "Robert of Flanders" of the Prologue is a son of Peter who became Emperor after his mother's death (which followed shortly upon that of her husband). He was crowned in 1221 and reigned till his death in 1228 when his brother Baldwin II, the last Latin emperor (1228–1261), succeeded him.

Thus the "daughter" of Robert is really his sister (and Baldwin's), Agnes by name. And it was not to Aragon that her father, Peter de Courtenay, was sending her, along with her mother, but to Constantinople. He decided to send them by sea while he chose to take the land route over the famous Via Egnatia. The two ladies put in to a port in northwestern Morea, not far from the castle of Beauvoir, and were received with honor by the elder Geoffrey de Villehardouin, still reigning in Morea—not by his son Geoffrey, as the Prologue states. Yolande and Geoffrey I together arranged the match between the younger Geoffrey and Agnes as a state marriage of advantage to Morea and the Empire.

There is no record of any "wars and scandals" between Robert and Geoffrey II. As for the meeting in Vlachia (that is, Thessaly), it should be identified with the parliament at Ravennika, in central Greece, which was called by Emperor Henry in 1209 and at which Geoffrey I became Henry's vassal for Morea and Seneschal of the Empire. The Prologue is correct in stating that Robert officially recognized Geoffrey II as Prince of Achaia. But the suzerainty over the islands of the Archipelago—along with that over Euboea and Boudonitza—was received by the same Geoffrey from Baldwin II in 1236, as a reward for his decisive aid to his brother-in-law in the defense of Constantinople in that year.

1

THIS IS THE BEGINNING OF THE USAGES OF THE EMPIRE OF ROMANIA. HOW THE PRINCE MUST DO HOMAGE TO THE EMPEROR.

In the first place, by the aforementioned Usages, the Prince of Achaia, the present as well as the future one, must do liege homage and fealty to the above-said Emperor of Constantinople, and must swear an oath in the presence of his barons, his faithful liegemen and his other subjects, that he shall protect and defend and to the full extent of his power shall secure the maintenance and defense by his officials of all the franchises and usages of the Empire of Romania.

2

And after the Prince has taken the oath to his barons, as is stated above, the said barons and liegemen are required to do homage, ligeance and fealty to the said Prince. And the others who hold fiefs must do homage; and the other subjects must take an oath of fealty. But if the Prince wishes that the said oath be taken through his procurator or procurators, or if he should not be in the Principality, then none of his subjects need do him homage or take an oath.

3 [1]

THE MANNER IN WHICH A VASSAL SHOULD ACT WHEN HE BECOMES A LIEGEMAN OF HIS LORD.

When a vassal becomes the liegeman of his lord, he should say: "Sire, I become your liegeman for this fief" (and he names the fief for which he is doing homage); "and I promise to keep and protect you as my lord against all persons, and against everything

[1] This whole chapter is copied from Jean d'Ibelin, *Assises de Jérusalem*, chapters CXCV–CXCVI.

which can live and die." And the lord should reply: "And I receive you in the faith of God and in mine." And he should kiss him on the mouth in sign of faith. But if he or she who does homage, as is above said, to the chief lord, has previously performed liege homage to another lord or lady, who may or may not be a vassal of the chief lord, he must save him in doing homage. And the reason is that no one who is another's man can afterward do homage to somebody else, if he does not first save his first lord, or unless he does it with his leave and consent; otherwise, he would be false in the fealty to him whose man he was first. And he who performs homage to another than the chief lord for anything which is in his land must do it in the above-described manner. For one cannot do homage except to one lord, since a man cannot perform more than one ligeance without great wrong-doing.[2] *And a man who does homage to another than the one of whom he is a liegeman is bound to his lord by the fealty which he pays him and by the homage which he does to him, to protect and guard him against all persons, and against everything which can live and die: and this does he promise him in doing homage. And from this it appears that he is bound never to raise his hand against the body or the person* [*of his lord*], *nor, in so far as he is able, may he consent or suffer that another should do it; nor is he to take or cause to be taken anything from his lord or from him whose liegeman he is. Nor should any man or woman act as counsel against his lord, unless the lord has appointed him counsel; nor should a man or woman speak words in court* [*against the lord*], *unless it is as his counsel; for if he does so, he places himself in the mediate or final judgment* [*of the court*] *with respect to things which are against the lord. Nor should he bear arms against his lord, to whom he is bound in fealty.*

[2] This sentence seems to contradict what has just been stated, namely, that liege homage can properly be done to more than one lord, provided the previous homage or homages are reserved. But in limiting liege homage to a single occasion, Ibelin has in mind the *Assise sur la ligece* of King Amaury (see Commentary: "Feudal Contract," VI), by which, strictly interpreted, only one ligeance, that to the king, could be done. In practice, however, the Jerusalemite vassal did liege homage to many lords, with the proper reservations. In his next sentence, the phrase "than the one of whom he is a liegeman" again refers to the theoretical single ligeance done to the king. For the entire discussion that follows is a description of the obligations of the vassal and the lord to whom he is most closely bound—his immediate or "natural" lord.

Nor should he to his knowledge bring about the shame or damage of his lord nor within his power allow or consent that another may do so. Neither should he violate the body of the lady or daughter of his lord nor lie with them in carnal intercourse unless it be in marriage, nor with the lord's sister so long as she is a maiden in the house of his lord; nor should he suffer anyone else to do so. And he should loyally give counsel to his lord in that in which he shall ask counsel.

Neither should the lord raise his hand nor cause another hand to be raised against the person of his vassal or against his fief unless it is done by the mediate or final judgment of his court. And the lord is bound to his liegeman by the fealty which exists between them in all things heretofore said by which the man is bound to his lord and the lord to him; because between the lord and his man there is fealty, and fealty should be common to both in respect of all the things said above. And each one must preserve his fealty to the other firmly and completely. And the vassal is so much the more bound to his lord in that he must enter into hostageship in order to release his lord from prison, if he is requested to do so by his lord or through his messages. And every man is held, by his fealty to his lord, if he finds him in need of arms, on foot, in the midst of his enemies, or in any place wherein he stands in danger of death, to use all his power to place him on a horse and rescue him from that peril. And if otherwise he is not able to do so, he must give him his own horse or whatever other [mount he has], if the lord requires it, and help him to mount. And whoever fails to do any of these things for his lord fails in his fealty to him. And if the lord can prove this by the record of the court, he can do to him and to his possessions as he should to a man who has failed in his fealty. But if he takes care to do any of these things for his lord, the lord is bound by his fealty through his loyal power to free him or those who have been made hostages for his liberation. In addition the man is bound to his lord to serve as a pledge for him to the full value of his fief. And he who fails his lord in this I believe should lose his fief as long as he shall live. And if a case should arise where the man serving as hostage or pledge for his lord should receive any damage through the said service, the lord is bound to make good to him every loss, and this through the fealty by which he is bound to him.

4

How the Prince Cannot Punish any Baron or Vassal of His Without the Consent of His Liegemen.

The Prince cannot punish any baron or vassal of his, either in civil or criminal action, nor injure him, nor place a penalty on him, without the counsel and consent of his liegemen or of the major part of them; nor render a decision concerning someone's fief or commission others to decide his actions at law; but he must render a decision through his liegemen. And the said lord or his officials cannot have any jurisdiction; but, in petty actions, like the matter of the vineyard of a fief or [the disposition] of a serf, the lord can entrust the judgment to his liegemen if the parties agree. And the lord cannot by force place any liegeman in any office against his will, nor punish him, nor retain his fief, unless it is with the judgment of his other liegemen.

5

How No Liegeman Can Be Held by His Lord Except for Two Causes.

It has been ordered in the said Usages that no liegeman of the Principality can be detained in person by his lord for any reason except these two, to wit: for the causes of homicide and treason. And it is thus because his fief provides his security.

6

What Should Be Done if a Liegeman Commits Homicide or Treason?

If it should happen that a liegeman has committed homicide or treason, what should be done? To this the answer is, that according to the customs and usages aforesaid the lord cannot punish or detain him unless the homicide or treason has first been proved and unless the judgment has been made in the case of the said liegeman by the other liegemen of the Principality. The lord can neither detain nor seize nor take his goods except by the judgment of the liegemen of the Principality.

7

AND IF IT HAPPENS THAT THE LORD HAS ONE OF HIS VASSALS, THAT IS, A FIEF OF ONE OF THEM, UNJUSTLY SEIZED, WHAT SHOULD BE DONE?

It is further asked, if the lord has the fief of one of his vassals seized unjustly, and this vassal of his has thrice asked for it in one year in the presence of his liegemen (if he can have such), demanding of him that he should return his fief and requesting the judgment of his court, and if the lord does not have the fief returned in full seizin when a year has passed, the homage for this fief passes to the nearest superior lord. And the vassal should first make a request for his fief within forty days, otherwise he shall lose the produce and revenues of that year. This same decision applies to others who have vassals subject to them if these vassals are liegemen. The man of simple homage has no court and can hold none. The liegeman or the man of simple homage shall be able to lodge a complaint before the overlord of his lord for the feudal goods which might have been taken from him unjustly by his lord; and he does this through a procurator appointed to this task.

8

When a criminal, civil, or feudal action arises between the Prince or another lord and one of his vassals, the Prince or the lord involved in the dispute must delegate one of his liegemen, or one not a liege, in his place. And the lord is required to rise, to give the delegate his baton and to leave the council, in accordance with the custom. And the delegate is to give the counsel of the liegemen of his court as much to the lord as to the party, retaining with him those liegemen who should appear to him most necessary in order to decide the question. And this is understood if the litigant is a liegeman.

9

No official of the Prince has any jurisdiction over freemen or their possessions, except the captain of a castellany over the liegemen of the castellany. Neither the Prince nor any official of his can deprive anyone of his possession, or seize his possession, after it has been held in seizin a year and a day, without judgment of his Court. But can the heir of the possessor who has been in possession for a year [and a day] be despoiled of the possession without judgment? The answer is no, unless it is for service required and not given.

10

The Prince can unite the fief of one castellany to that of another and augment or diminish the fiefs when they are in his hands. And he can give them to whom it pleases him. And he can grant the fief for a service less than that which the said fief owes. But can the other liegemen do such a thing? The answer is no, if there is a diminution of service.

11

The Prince can grant of his own feudal land and even of his domain, without service, for some rental. And if the aforesaid lord should make a grant without any rental, what shall happen? Some say that the grant made without a rental has no validity, and a much greater [number of people] of the country say that the rental should be given. Others say that the grant is valid during the life of the grantor. And the lord can grant land which is to return to his hands, even during the lifetime of those who hold the said land for life. And if someone holds land for the legitimate descendants of his body and he has no heir, and it visibly appears that he can have no descendants of his body, the lord can, while the possessor is still alive, grant the said lands to whomever it pleases him to possess them after the death of the present possessor, writing in such case in the letter [of grant]: "if he who at present holds the land shall die without heirs of his body." And such a grant shall be valid if he who is in possession dies during the life of the grantor or of his heirs. And if the grantor is a woman, the letter should state that she makes the grant for herself and for her heirs. More, the said grant shall be valid if the grantor places him to whom he gives it in possession of a part of the granted fief. But if the Prince simply grants the land to somebody without stating: "for him and his heirs," it should be understood that the donation does not pass to the heirs of him who receives it, but must return to the heirs of the grantor.

12

No vassal of any baron, and no knight or whoever else it may be, is required to show the Prince how he holds his land of his lord, except if his lord has been previously dispossessed by a judgment. And if a question should be raised to a vassal concerning any fief, he is not held to answer if his lord is not required to; moreover, the lord is bound to defend him upon the request of his vassal.

13

The Prince or another lord can hold court with those liegemen whom he can have. But in truth if the party who brings action asks and requests that the lord have more liegemen, the lord is bound to comply, and, according to the importance of the case, the court must be provided and established.

14

And if the Prince or another lord has seized the land of any baron, knight, or vassal of his, he cannot seize the holding of any vassals of the baron, but he can by right keep their service for himself. And this is to be understood, whether the land has been justly or unjustly seized.

15

And when the Prince has been taken by enemies, which God forbid, and it is possible to ransom him, he can for his ransom place his liegemen in hostageship until the money for his ransom has been raised; and, once the money has been raised, the lord is bound to release his liegemen or to give other hostages in their place to the enemy. However, he cannot otherwise place them in hostageship against their will.

16

If a castellany or a complete fief of the Principality has been taken by enemies, which God forbid, and this castellany or fief has vassals, these vassals can require their lord to come to their aid in the dangers to which their life is exposed. And if the lord does not assist them, the vassals are not bound to give him any service for the lost fiefs, except if they have recovered them.

17

If the lord wishes to send any of his barons or liegemen outside the Principality on a mission that pertains to the common interest of the Principality, he is bound to obey the wish of the lord, receiving from him his expenses. But if he [the lord] wishes to send him in his own interest, he cannot do so against the will [of his vassal].

18

If someone commits treason against his lord and after the act of treason makes a grant to someone, and if it happens that he dies before he has been proceeded against by judgment for his iniquities, the grant is valid. And if he dies before being disinherited by judgment of the court of his superior, his son or nearest relative should succeed to his goods, as he should have succeeded if the event had not occurred, just as happened to Sire Nicholas of Tremolay, who was a traitor; and because he was not disinherited during his lifetime, after his death Sire Aymon of Rens and the lady Margaret of Cephalonia succeeded to a fief called Micopoli.[1]

19

If the Prince has a castle on an enemy frontier, he cannot pledge it to the enemy or destroy it without the counsel and consent of his liegemen.

[1] Micopoli was part of the barony of Chalandritsa, which was located in the north-central part of Morea.

20

The Prince or whoever else it may be cannot give up the liege homage which must be made to him, against the wish of the liegeman; but with the latter's consent he may. And as for that of a man of simple homage he can do so in his own wish and give it up to suit his good pleasure. The lord cannot give the ligeance of his liegeman to anyone of inferior station to that of his liege vassal, unless he grants the castellany in which the vassal has liege land.

21

When the Prince gives a fief to a person and after some time there arises a dispute between the lord and the vassal concerning either the appurtenances to or any part of the fief, if he to whom the fief has been given is found to be in seizin, the proof rests upon the lord; and the reverse is true if the fief-holder is not found to be in seizin. And this is understood if the lord has not proved that the part in question pertains to another fief, since, in this case, the proof rests upon the vassal.

22

The Prince cannot separate the liegeman from his vassals in the performance of service, unless the liegeman consents to it (and rightly, because he can and ought to have more confidence in his own men than in strangers). And the lord cannot order a baron or liegeman to serve in any place if he does not send him accompanied with a reasonable company and in accordance with the needs and necessities of the place to which he is sending him. (And this is quite a reasonable thing.)

23

By the Usage and Custom of the Empire of Romania, the Prince cannot place upon his vassals or freemen, or even on their serfs, any tallages or collections on any condition or under any name whatever, or anything, for the utility of the country, without the counsel and consent as well of the liegemen and vassals as of the other freemen. And in this case, those who consent are under obligation, and those who do not consent are under none. But in truth, if he wishes to marry his daughter or ransom himself from his enemies when he has been taken by them, in this case he can levy a collection only on the men of simple homage. Moreover, the lord should take care that no vassal, baron, or soldier allows straw, poultry, or any other thing to be taken by force from the serfs of his subjects.

24

When the Prince commands that a fief be seized on the ground of service required, and then not given to him, he can confiscate the service of the serfs of this fief. But he cannot take the produce that has been or is about to be gathered. And when the vassal offers the lord the service within forty days, the lord is bound to restore the fief to him in full seizin, except the service of the serfs. And if the vassal delays in rendering the service to the lord beyond the forty days, the lord shall take a proportionate amount of the produce to compensate for the service defaulted, according to the value of the revenues of the fief or fiefs. And if he delays for a year and a day in giving the service, he loses the fief, except if the heir appears offering the service, or the ward, whose rights are not prejudiced. And the declaration is never to be made by judgment of court, save if the vassal is detained by a legitimate hindrance, of which fact he is then required to notify the lord, if he can, within the year.[1]

25

How Only the Prince Can Maintain and Make Free a Serf.

Only the Seignior, that is the Prince, can maintain and make free his serf or that of another, with the consent of the lord of the serf. And the Seignior can give a fief to the Church or part of a fief, or even a serf. But if the donation is made by someone else, it shall be valid only during the lifetime of the donor.

[1] What is meant by "declaration" in the last sentence? The context seems to require "of confiscation" after "declaration," but it is difficult to believe that the confiscation of the fief is extra-judicial. The opposite course of judgment of peers is too repeatedly emphasized in the Assizes (arts. 4, 6, 18, 69), and for more serious derelictions than default of service (as in art. 167).

26

How Long a Delay Is Permitted a Vassal in Preparing Himself to Render Service Due.

When the lord commands a vassal to render service due, the vassal is to have at least fifteen days in which to prepare himself. However, if a castle is being besieged, or the lord [himself], each vassal is required to give aid as soon as he can, and especially those who are held to some service. And the same shall prevail if a general expedition is made by the Prince in the enemy country, or if an enemy army invades the country and the lands of the Prince.

27

How the Vassal Can Be Excused from Giving Counsel in the Court.

If the lord requests a vassal to give counsel in his court, or personal service, or any other reasonable thing, and the said vassal is legitimately detained, [the lord] must hold him as excused.

28

When the Prince Makes War on One of His Barons, What Should the Vassals of This Baron Do?

If the Prince makes war on one of his barons or vassals, the vassals of that baron or vassal are held to defend their lord if the Prince has unjustly begun the war. Further, the said baron or vassal is bound to request the lord once, twice, or three times that he must abstain from this molestation; and he should do this in the presence of his barons and of his liegemen, if he can have a sufficient number of these; if he cannot have them, then before and in the presence of other men worthy of faith. And if he [the Prince] is not willing to abstain, the vassals are bound to defend their lord, and they can do so without penalty. But if he began the war justly, the sub-vassals are not bound to defend their lord against the higher lord if they have done homage, reserving their fealty to the superior; otherwise, they are bound to defend him until by judgment of court he shall be disinherited.

29

How the Lord Can Constrain a Vassal to Maintain Mounted Service.

The lord can constrain his vassal to maintain service on horse if the vassal has a knight's fief and if the fief is in such a state that it can support mounted service. But if the fief has been wasted by war to the point where it cannot support mounted service, he cannot be constrained, but he must serve the lord in person, the service being reduced in proportion as the fief has been diminished by war. But if the fief is not a knight's fief, no matter how great its value, it must not be constrained to supply service on horse, even though the father of the vassal had been a knight.

30

How the Liegeman, or the Liegewoman, Can Grant a Third of the Fief.

It is also contained in the Usages of the Empire that a liegeman or liegewoman can freely grant a third of his or her fief or fiefs to him or to those whom they wish, with the service due for that land. But he cannot sell it without the consent of his lord. A man of simple homage cannot grant either a third or fourth part, nor a serf nor any land without permission of his lord, from whom he holds the land.

And the lord cannot constrain any liegeman to accept an office against his will.

31

How a Liegewoman, After the Death of Her Husband, Can Marry Whom it Pleases Her, Except an Enemy.

In addition, it is contained in the said Usages that a liegewoman, her husband being dead, can marry whom she will so long as she does not marry an enemy, giving the lord the third part of the annual revenues of the land that she holds of the lord as a liege, or the value of the revenues, that is, of one-third of them; and this [she pays] as her relief. The woman of simple homage cannot marry without the permission of her lord, if the lord commanded her when he invested her with the fief that she should not marry without his leave: in which case she is not to do so. But if she marries before she has been prohibited, she incurs no penalty. And if after the prohibition shall have been made, she does marry, the penalty is at the wish of the lord. But truly, the lord cannot give her in marriage against her will.

32

How Fiefs and Baronies Are Inherited by Primogeniture.

In truth, in a fief, a barony, or in the Principality the first-born succeeds the father or the mother and if there is no son or daughter, the nearest relative who appears in the Principality succeeds, if he is of the line from which the paternal or maternal fief proceeds. And if a fief dates from the conquest of the Principality, the nearest relative, however remote, succeeds, provided always that he is of the paternal or maternal family. In the case of a paternal or maternal fief, the son or daughter, after the death of the father or of the mother, retains possession even without authority or permission from the superior, provided he is in the Principality. But if he is outside the Principality, he cannot acquire the possession without the authority of his superior. In the case of the transmission or succession to others [than the son or daughter], in order to acquire the succession, it is necessary to await the authority of the superior lord. What shall happen if one relative is of the third degree and a descendant of the female line, and another is of the fourth degree and is a descendant of the male line? The answer is that he of the third degree is to succeed, since he is the nearer.

33 [1]

For What Reasons a Liegeman of the Prince Can Be Held.

It has been ordered in the said Usages that a liegeman of the Prince cannot be detained in person by the lord except for two reasons, that is, for homicide and for treason, for his fief provides his security.

[1] This article repeats chapter 5 above, with only a slight change in wording.

34

How, After the Death of the Father, the Son, if He Is of Legal Age, Does Not Pay Relief for the Investiture of the Fief of His Father but Does for That of His Mother.

Of common accord it was laid down that if after the death of the father the son is of legal age, he does not pay relief when he is invested with the fief of his father, but he does for that of his mother. All the others pay every time the fief is changed, except that if the son is in wardship, the guardian does not pay relief; and when the son is invested with the fief after he has attained legal age, he does not pay relief if his lord has had the wardship; otherwise, he pays for the goods received by his guardian. In the escheats, in truth, which belong to a male, relief is not paid, but it is in those belonging to a liegewoman. And if a liege daughter succeeds her father or her mother, even if she has a husband, when she is invested with the fief of her father or her mother, she pays relief. And when a liegewoman marries, she likewise pays relief. And for like reason when her husband dies and she is invested with the fief, even if the fief has been inherited by the woman, she pays. Likewise, she pays when she is invested with her dower fief. And when a man or woman of simple homage marries, he or she does not pay relief. And if a liegeman or liegewoman has a holding of simple homage, he or she does not pay relief for this land, but only for the liege land. It is asked whether, whenever a husband of a woman dies, she should be reinvested with a fief of which she has already been invested, even though this fief is her inheritance. The answer is yes.

35

How Much Should a Liegewoman or One of Simple Homage Have for Her Dower After the Death of Her Husband.

According to the Usages of the Empire of Romania, a woman of liege or of simple homage, after the death of her husband, should have as her dower, or her dot, half of the fief or fiefs, of the castle or castles, and half of the jurisdiction of her husband which he possessed when they entered into matrimony, provided that they occupied the same bed on at least one occasion. Of his inheritances [which fell to him during their marriage], in truth, she has nothing; but of the acquisitions which the husband made during their marriage she is to have half, if she survives her husband. But if the husband survives his wife, the sons of this wife, born of the first husband, do not succeed to anything. And if she has sons by a first husband and survives her husband, then the son of the first husband succeeds to his acquisitions, unless she has a male heir by him who made the acquisitions, since it is he who succeeds. But if the son of the second husband, that is, of the one who acquired the land, dies before his mother, the son of the first husband succeeds to the acquisition of the mother even if the son of the second husband has sons. And a liegewoman, no longer having a husband, can give a third of her acquisitions to the second son of her daughter or to whomever it pleases her. But what happens if a man has not paid his wife's relief during her life? Should it not be proper that he or his executors pay? The answer is that the husband or his executors are bound to pay the relief from the time that the husband has had the seizin of his wife's land. If a husband invests his wife with a certain quantity of money, not mentioning that he has invested her with half of his land, what happens after the husband's death? Shall she not receive the dower of her husband's land or his acquisitions? The answer is that she shall have only the acquisitions, since he has already invested her with the money. And it shall be thus if anyone says: "I take this lady as my wife, stipulating and establishing this contract"; since in this case the contract shall be observed, and she shall not have the acquisitions, unless the contrary has been stated in the contract. But what shall happen if a liege wife acquires a holding? Shall the husband have no part in this acquisition? Some answer yes, others say the opposite. But if she is a wife of simple homage, then what shall happen? The reply is: the same thing, according to some, if the fief is free; and others say the opposite.

36

HOW WHEN A FIEF IS VACANT HE WHO IS TO SUCCEED MUST ASK FOR IT WITHIN FORTY DAYS.

When a fief is vacant, to which several are eligible to succeed, he who has the right to the said fief must ask for it within forty days, otherwise he loses the products of that year. And if he does not ask for it within a year and a day, during which time he is in the Principality, he loses it, even if some hindrance legitimately prevented him, and the nearest heir of the deceased shall succeed him if he asks for the fief within the year and a day after the death of the lord of the fief. And if he is outside of the Principality, he has a time limit of two years and two days: and whenever he shall appear within this term and shall offer homage, the land must be assigned to him. Such limits must be observed even if the feudal inheritance amounts to no more than a serf or a little feudal land. This is what happened to the mother of Sire Nicholas, formerly Marshal of the Principality, who lost the barony of Matagrifon, when she was in the prison of Michael Palaiologos, as some say, and was thus dispossessed.[1]

[1] The contest over the barony of Akova or Matagrifon in Arcadia, the largest fief of Morea, is the most famous case in the history of the Principality. The mother of Nicholas III de St. Omer, "formerly Marshal of the Principality," was Marguerite de Passavant, the daughter of John II de Neuilly, hereditary Marshal and Baron of Passavant, who had married a daughter of Gautier I de Rosières, the lord of Akova. In 1262, when William de Villehardouin was released by Michael Palaiologos (see Introduction, pp. 5–6), Marguerite and another lady of high rank were sent to Constantinople as hostages for the Prince. During their absence, Marguerite fell heir to the barony of Akova when her uncle, Gautier II de Rosières, died without direct heirs. William took possession of the barony when Marguerite failed to appear within the legal period for claiming it—a year and day, says the Greek Chronicle (l. 7331). The fact that Marguerite was unable to appear because she was abroad in the service of her lord was an unavailing argument when the case was argued in 1276 in the High Court of the Principality. The case was not judged on grounds of equity but in the strictest technical fashion: William cited two chapters from the "book of usages" (corresponding to articles 15 and 36) that required the vassal to serve as hostage for the lord and to claim an inheritance within a certain period. Despite the "legitimate hindrance" of being a hostage abroad Marguerite lost her case. The provision at the end of article 3, borrowed from Ibelin, which requires the lord to compensate the vassal who suffers some damage while serving as hostage, could hardly have been a part of Moreot law in 1276, for Ibelin composed his treatise only in

37

How All Freemen Can Make a Will, Stipulating Certain Things.

All of the liege vassals and those of simple homage and other freemen of the Principality aforesaid, both men and women, can freely make and order a testament of their movable and immovable bourgeois holdings, stipulating the following: that if the grain that [the deceased] caused to be sown in his feudal land or in that of his wife has sprouted, or grapes have been formed, or the olives or the fruits of the trees have been formed, all should belong to the deceased. And neither the lord nor the heirs of the fief may take the *zemuro* [1] of the land described above as sown. But the lord or he who is to inherit the said fief does, on the other hand, take the *zemuro* of the products of other sowings he has made in this place. To be sure, the fruits of this land which have not been harvested belong to the lord or to the heir of the fief. The year in which there begins for feudal goods [2] . . . begins when the olives and the acorns are gathered, that is, after the feast of the Exaltation of the Holy Cross [September 14].

1265–66. The account of the case in the Chronicle of Morea (Greek Chronicle, ll. 7301–7752; French Chronicle, pars. 501–31, pp. 197–211) is one of the most valuable descriptions of procedure in all the legal literature of feudalism.

It is clear from the Chronicle's account that William seized upon a technical excuse in order to acquire a very coveted barony. He confesses after the case that he was responsible for Marguerite's inability to put in her claim on time and that he had planned to reward her by giving her half of the barony and bestowing the other half on his own younger daughter Marguerite; but the haughty demeanor of the powerful St. Omer brothers angered him and he agreed to reopen the case and defeat Marguerite's claims by citing the "book of the usages of the land." (Cp. Greek Chronicle, ll. 7620–72.) Having won, he would still be generous and grant Marguerite one-third of the barony. The other two-thirds went to his daughter. The simple fact is that William was strong enough to impose his will upon the High Court.

It is possible that the limit of two years and two days stated in art. 36 was a new regulation that resulted from the Passavant case.

---

[1] *Zemuro* is from the Greek *geōmoron* or *gēmoron*, meaning the portion of the crop given by the cultivator to the proprietor of the land. See also art. 214.

[2] There is a lacuna at this point in the manuscripts.

38

WHEN A MAN DIES INTESTATE, HIS WIFE SUCCEEDS TO THE BOURGEOIS GOODS, MOVABLE AND IMMOVABLE.

If a man dies intestate, his wife inherits the bourgeois goods, movable and immovable; but if he has no wife the son inherits; and if there are sons or daughters, all inherit equally. And if no sons or daughters appear, the nearest relative inherits; and if of near relatives none is found in the Principality, the goods are to be held by the lord for a year and a day in expectation of the appearance from elsewhere of a cousin or near relative; and if such a one appears, the goods of the deceased must be given to him; and if no one appears, the lord is required to distribute the goods for the repose of the soul of the deceased. In this type of cases males and females succeed equally if they are of the same degree; and let it be understood that unmarried, and not married, daughters are involved, because the latter cannot ask for anything after their marriage save if they are willing to return to the total of the inheritance the dot which they received and then share the whole. This, according to some.

39

When a liegeman or a man of simple homage dies, the mother has the wardship of the son or daughter. And if the mother dies first, the father has the wardship. But if both the father and mother die, in this case he who is to succeed to the fief shall have the wardship, whether he is the lord of the land or a cousin. And he is bound to provide sustenance and clothes for the ward whose guardian he is. And the guardian, whoever he may be, must render homage by reason of the wardship. And he must ask for the wardship within the proper time, as if he were to succeed to the fief; else he loses the wardship of this land. And he must present the ward whose guardian he is. And if he does not present the ward, the lord is not bound to give him the wardship. And if he was not able to make the presentation and nevertheless was invested with the wardship, that should be valid, as if the presentation had been made. And that which one guardian does cannot be revoked by another guardian, but the heir can revoke it when he shall be invested with the fief. And if the boy or girl does not wish to remain with the guardian, he need not do so, according to some, if he has reached his seventh year; otherwise, he must remain with his guardian. But cannot the mother or father order that the boy or girl be reared with other people than the guardian of the land? The answer is that, according to others, they can rightfully do or order this, but the guardian need not provide the living expenses, if he does not so wish, from the time that the boy or girl does not reside with him. And if the boy or girl does not wish to remain with the guardian, he can live with the nearest relative while being supported by the guardian. And the vassals of a child in wardship do not need to render homage to the guardian, save if the guardian has been the husband of a woman who had vassals, or if the guardian is he who should succeed after the ward's death; in any case, when homage is done, the fealty to the ward, who is to inherit upon arriving at the lawful age, must be reserved. Furthermore, if the lord has the wardship of the ward but is not to succeed him, or if another cousin, who also is not in the line of succession, has the wardship, or if it is the nearest relative and he should neglect to claim the wardship or should renounce it, [then] no [one of these] shall receive the homage of the vassals of the ward. But what happens in the case of a father who has the wardship of his son for the maternal fief?

40

If a father, or a mother who has no husband, wishes to divest himself of a fief in order that the son may make a dower for his wife, and if the son should die after the divestiture and after he had been invested and should not leave any legitimate heirs descended of his body, none of the cousins of the son can inherit, whether on the paternal or maternal side, except in the case of a fief which has been acquired. Further, if the father or mother who wishes to divest himself does so before the lord on this condition—that if the son dies leaving no legitimate heirs of his body, the other cousins can inherit—in this case the cousins of the son whether on the paternal or maternal side can inherit just as they should have done in the first instance if the divestiture had not taken place; but it is necessary that the lord consent to his divestiture. And if someone divests himself of his fief and it is not in the presence of his lord, this is not valid. But if the divestiture is performed in the presence of the vicar of the lord, what shall then happen? The answer is that it is valid since it occurs every day.

41

It is further contained in the Usages of the Empire of Romania that when any land or fief falls [to one], to which the wife succeeds or ought to succeed, the wife and not the husband should present herself. And if the wife neglects to put forth her claim within the period prescribed above, she loses her right, and those who according to the Usages ought to succeed do so. Furthermore, no passage of time during her marriage prejudices her in the fief with which she is invested. But after the death of her husband, she is to observe the time limits prescribed above. What shall happen if the wife presents herself without her husband? The answer is that she must be received.

42

All the vassals and men of simple homage of the Principality of Achaia can have jurisdiction over the civil cases of their serfs; and the serfs cannot appeal to any person through any means.

43

The exercise of high justice is proper only to the peers of the Prince, namely, the Duke of Athens, the lord of Naxos, the triarchs of Negroponte, the lord of Boudonitza, the count of Cephalonia, the lord of Karytaina, the lords of Patras and of Matagrifon, the marshal, as long as he is in the army and in authority over the soldiers, and the lord of Kalavryta, who was a de Tournay.

What happens if the serf of a vassal wishes to bring a charge against another serf of the same lord in a civil case? Cannot the lord of the serf require of him that he must not commit the case to anyone other than himself and that it must be placed before him and not another? The answer is yes, according to some. Further, if the serf brings a complaint against the other serf before the suzerain of his lord, the second serf is bound to reply notwithstanding that his lord had forbidden him this. Others say the contrary if the lord of the serf is a liegeman; and the reason is that he has a court for his serfs and vassals.

44

If the husband of a vassal has been captured or is absent, and he succeeds to a fief or part of a fief or to a wardship, the vassal, his wife, can present herself before the lord of the fief and receive the investiture or the wardship, notwithstanding the absence of her husband. And after the return of the husband, she shall present him before her lord as her guardian.

45

If a vassal marries a woman, and his mother or stepmother holds half of his fief or fiefs, his wife after the death of her husband shall have no dower of that land. And the reason is that she is to have no dower except in the land which her husband possessed when they both entered into matrimony.

46

If he wishes, a liegeman or liegewoman can grant the third part of his fief or fiefs to whomever it pleases him without asking the lord, provided that he has had seizin for forty days; but he cannot sell his fiefs. And this, indeed, if he acquired the fiefs together and from one lord. But if he has first acquired and possessed one fief and later another from another lord, in this case he shall be able to grant only a third part of each fief. And if he succeeds to several fiefs which he holds from one lord or from several, he can grant only a third part of each fief. And if he grants an entire fief, he forfeits all of it, and the same superior lord acquires this fief. And if he grants two-thirds, the superior lord takes that which he has granted in excess, and the recipient acquires the third part of the fief.

47

If feudal land is granted to someone, and in the letters of the grant the recipient is not specified to be a liegeman, it is understood that the grant is in simple homage.

48

When judgment is to be made in matters which relate to the service of free vassals, as in matters respecting fiefs, like criminal or civil cases, in obtaining the judgment only liegemen have a voice, along with prelates who have baronies in the said Principality.

And the barons are judged by the other barons as liegemen, their superior nevertheless standing above them.

And some say that like the bishops in the Principality the commanders of the Hospital of Saint John and of the house of Mostenitsa [1] have a voice.

49

The barons and other knights and liege vassals can, with their lieges, have jurisdiction over the fiefs of their vassals. In truth, if they have seized the land of their vassals unjustly, and if they fail to restore it to them in full seizin, the vassal is not bound to receive it. And if the lord has withheld it from his vassal for a year and a day, after the year has passed, the homage passes at once to the nearest superior lord, provided that the vassal has requested his lord three times during the year to make restitution, demanding judgment by his court. And the first request must be made within forty days; otherwise, the vassal loses the produce of that year; and this is understood to apply to liegemen. But the man of simple homage, when his lord acts against him, is able to complain and bring suit after forty days before the lord of his lord, after having previously requested his lord to do justice within those forty days. But when a vassal brings suit against his lord within the year before the lord of his lord, he loses his fief if he is a liegeman and it

[1] The "house of Mostenitsa" was the military-religious order of the Teutonic Knights, whose headquarters were at Mostenitsa, located in southwestern Peloponnesus.

is a question of the entire fief. But if the question involves movable property, he can lodge his complaint at once.

50

If a liegeman has granted an entire fief acquired at the conquest of the Principality or inherited by him, a fief which according to the aforementioned Usages he cannot grant, he to whom it is granted acquires a third of the fief, and the rest reverts to the principal lord for the lifetime of the grantor. And after the death of the grantor his heir succeeds, his son or whatever other heir it may be, provided that he presents himself within a year and has offered service during the life of the lord to whom he is bound, affirming that he is ready to render to the principal lord the service owed by the land.

51

If a lord has seized the land of one of his vassals for service required but not given, and the vassal has failed to perform the service within a year and a day, the land remains to the lord after the year and a day have passed, save if he who is to succeed has presented himself, offering the service due. And the service having been offered, the lord is obliged to give the land to him.

52

When the lord grants someone a certain feudal holding, promising to complete a certain fief—either an entire fief or part of a fief, if the lord dies without having fulfilled his promise, the vassal is not required to perform any service until the service which he should perform for the land is determined by the successor of the said lord. Moreover, the successor of the lord is not required to complete the fief, or a part thereof, if he does not wish. But the heir is required to do so if it is contained in the letters of the grant that the grantor gives it on behalf of himself and his heirs. And if the lord has diminished the fief of his vassal, the said vassal is not required to render service to his lord for the fief thus diminished until it has been restored to him entire.

53

If someone holds the wardship of a minor whose land owes personal service, the guardian, by reason of this wardship, is required to serve in person, unless he himself is bound to serve personally for his own land.

54

The lord of whom the fief is held can invest the ward who is to succeed to the fief, by grace, before the ward reaches legal age, so long as the guardian's rights to receive the fruits of the fief are not prejudiced. And if the said ward should wish to marry someone, he can dower her with this fief, just as if he were of legal age. If the lord is the guardian, he shall restore the land to the ward, or if anyone else has been the guardian of the minor, he shall restore the land to him, when the superior lord concedes the majority of the minor.

55

How the Fief Is Not to Be Diminished if the Liegeman Is Not Able to Give the Service Which He Owes the Lord.

The liegeman who has feudal land for which he is bound to his lord in service, even personal service, if he cannot perform the service because the fief is diminished by war or because he must depart for some other legitimate cause, can lawfully commend the land to the above-mentioned lord for two years and two days, or less, if he wishes. And he can recover it within the said period, if he wishes, by offering the service owed. But if, after the said period of two years and two days has passed, he does not offer the service owed, he loses the land, unless he who is to succeed to the land offers the service to the lord within a year and a day or unless the lord has taken the land in commendation and has accepted it, because in this case the vassal does not undergo any risk of loss, even if ten years elapse. It is understood that the vassal in this case commends his land to the lord when the lord does not wish to give him permission to leave for a lawful reason. Because otherwise, if he has permission, it is not necessary that he commend his land.

56

How the Husband Cannot by Testament Deprive His Wife Either of Her Bed or of Her Clothes.

The husband cannot deprive his wife either of her bed or of the clothes of her body by testament. But the wife shall have her bed furnished, that is, a mattress with a pillow and a curtain, and two quilts and two pairs of sheets, in each case according to the quality and means of each person, unless there exist contrary agreements. As for the clothing of the wife it remains to her if the goods of the husband suffice to pay the debts. And if they do not suffice, the wife is left with only two dresses and a silver girdle.

57

How the Principal Grantor Is Required to Carry Out the Offer He Makes While the Heir Is Not Held Thereto.

When a liegeman gives a fief or part of a fief to someone and promises him, if someone brings action against him regarding this land or takes it from him, that he and his heirs shall be held to restore it to him, the principal grantor is bound to carry out the promise, but the heir is not so bound. And if a liegeman gives somebody's fief which is vacant to someone else, after the death of the grantor, the recipient shall have nothing if he has not had the seizin of the fief. And what shall happen if he has been invested only with the hood? The answer is that this is not valid, because by the act of investiture the possession of a fief or part of a fief is not acquired, during the life of the grantor or of the heirs of the grantor. But what happens when it is so stated in the letters that he grants for himself and for his heirs?

58

When a Liegewoman Contracts a Marriage with One Who Has No Feudal Land and He Has Children by Her, Etc.

If a liegewoman contracts a marriage with someone who has no feudal land and has sons by him, if their son wishes to contract a legitimate marriage, his mother cannot divest herself of all or part of her land even with the consent of her husband, in order that her son may provide a dower for his wife, inasmuch as she is in the guardianship of her husband, unless the authorization and consent of the lord are given. But if the vicar gives his consent, should not that suffice? The answer and reply is that this does suffice according to some. But it is safer if this is done with the consent of the natural lord. And others say, perhaps more wisely, that even if the authorization of the lord has been given the act is not valid, because the wife is in the guardianship of her husband.

59

How the Lord Is Bound to Restore Land to Him Who Presents Himself Within a Year on Behalf of His Wife.

If a man possessing no feudal land marries a vassal and she has been negligent in rendering service to her lord, for the reason that her son-in-law or someone else who should succeed to the land has seized the land, the husband can present himself within the year, on behalf of his wife or of the succession, and offer the service owed: and the lord is bound to restore the land to him.

60

How the Lord Can Grant Permission to His Vassal to go Outside the Principality.

After a vassal has been invested with his fief, his lord can give him license to stay outside the Principality, as long as it shall please him, without any prejudice to the land with which he has been invested, although with prejudice to that with which he is yet to be invested, if he should not return within two years and two days. But if he should leave without license and should have no legitimate reason for being absent, and he who is to succeed to the fief should present himself within the limit of a year, the lord of the fief is bound to invest the latter. But if the vassal should leave with his lord's permission, in no circumstances can he who is present in the Principality present himself within a year, nor shall he be invested in the year following; and only after two years and two days have passed, shall he be placed in possession.

61

How the Sons of a Deceased Vassal Ought to be Invested.

If a vassal who has sons or daughters dies, whoever it may be of the sons or daughters present in the Principality can present himself to his lord and ask to be invested, offering the homage which he is obliged to give. And the lord shall invest him, son or daughter, whoever it may be, notwithstanding that the eldest sons or daughters are alive and absent from the Principality or that, even if they are present in it, they fail to appear before the lord of the fief during a year and a day. For the nearest relative must present himself within a year and a day.

62

Concerning the Vassal Who Has a Mother or a Stepmother.

A liege vassal or one of simple homage, having a mother or stepmother who possesses half of the fief of his father, by virtue of her dower, after the death of his mother or stepmother is not required to request the investiture of this inheritance from his lord, but he is indeed required to ask permission to enter into possession of the inheritance, and the lord is bound to grant the permission, nor is it necessary that he be placed in possession with the authority of the lord. And the tenants of the land of the mother or stepmother must render homage to the son or to his procurator, in accordance with the requirements of the land. But if the mother held the land through acquisition or inheritance, the son, after his mother's death, must ask to be invested and must render homage for that acquired or inherited land. And the tenants of the acquired land, after the investiture of the son, must similarly be invested by the son and render to him homage; and the same applies for inherited land.

63

A liegeman of a lord can render homage and ligeance to another lord only if he reserves his first ligeance. For truly, if he does not reserve his first ligeance, he loses the land of that ligeance. But shall a judgment of court be necessary? The answer is yes.

64

If two relatives of equal degree appear in order to take possession of an inheritance, the male shall be preferred to the female and the one born first to the one born afterwards.

65

All vassals who are bound to some service to their lord are not obliged to perform it outside the Principality, but throughout the Principality including its divisions, even if it is necessary to cross the sea. And if it happens that the vassal loses part of his fief or that it is taken by enemies, he must perform his service in proportionate amount. And if he loses all of it, his lord is bound to provide for him. And if he fails to provide for him, the vassal is not obliged to do any service. Furthermore, nobody can render homage of fealty through a procurator, but the lord can permit it as an act of grace, deputing someone to receive the homage in his place.

66

If a wife possesses a fief and with her husband, or by herself, has made a grant during their marriage, even with the consent of her husband or of her own son, shall the wife, after the death of her husband, be able to revoke the grant? Yes, if the fief is the inheritance of the wife or her dower.

67

When a vassal becomes a leper or through some other incurable bodily infirmity becomes incapacitated, he can serve through another knight, if he is a knight and is held to knight service. And if he cannot provide a knight, he is to present two squires. Indeed, if he is a squire he shall supply a squire, if his land is a sergeanty. If he is sick for a short time, he is not obliged to do any personal service. But if he is bound to the Court by some service other than a personal one, like supplying some men-at-arms, he must perform this at the request of the Court, that is, of the lord or of his captain.

68

Homage should be performed by a liegeman in the following way: the liegeman is to hold his hands joined and extended and to place them in the hands of his lord, saying that he becomes his liegeman. But if it is a woman, someone else shall speak for her, as is customary. But what shall happen if one owes liege homage for one fief and simple homage for another? The answer is that in the first case liege homage shall be done, and that afterwards an oath shall be sworn for the land held in simple homage, against all men who can live and die, to guard the person of the lord and of his wife and sons, and [to defend] his castles and his fief.

In this case [of liege homage], the lord must reply that he accepts his vassal as his liegeman, and he promises him to preserve and maintain his right; and then he kisses him and lastly invests him with the land, with a hood or a glove or with some other object. And liege homage must be done without any condition attached and must take place in the presence of at least two liegemen, so that these may testify to the ligeance if the need arises; otherwise the ceremony is not valid if there are no liegemen present. A man of simple homage does homage by taking an oath on the Book. A guardian does homage in the way that the fief of which he is guardian requires. And if a man of simple homage should do liege homage, he shall lose the land for which he did ligeance.

69

He who breaks [that is, forfeits] the seizin made by his lord in the cases elsewhere described, either by homicide, treason, or service required but not given, is disinherited from the time that this has been proven and judgment has been made by the Court. Otherwise, if the land is seized unjustly, he is not disinherited. Let it be understood [that this occurs] when he has not been taken; otherwise, if he has been taken, the land is not seized before sentence has been given and carried into execution, and the heir succeeds.

And if he has been a traitor, the land is not seized before the sentence has been made against him.

69 *bis*

The vassals of a lord are not bound to perform their service at the command of someone, if he has no order from the lord or his captain.

70

Be it understood that each liegeman who is held to annual service to someone for the land which he holds from him is to serve four months, if the lord wishes, in a castle, and four on a frontier; and he shall remain for four months in his house, or in any place where it shall appear to him to be more necessary in order to fulfill his service in the aforesaid Principality.

71

He, indeed, who obtains land by acquisition in the Principality and has no letter [of donation] is bound to serve throughout the year according to the stipulations set forth above, dividing the service into the three parts of the year, if he is a liegeman, and likewise if he is a man of simple homage. But as for a Greek lord, what shall he do, if he has little land or few serfs? The same, according to some, since [the terms of] this service are not stated.

72

This is the difference between a man of liege and one of simple homage: the lord can appoint a vassal of simple homage an official in an office of honor—a liegeman he cannot. And a man of simple homage is obliged to serve according to the terms of his letters. The liegeman belongs to the council of the lord while the man of simple homage does not. The liegeman can grant a third of his land while the man of simple homage cannot. A liegewoman can marry without securing her lord's permission, while giving a third of the produce yielded in the first year, or the equivalent value.

And a woman of simple homage cannot marry after this has been forbidden her by her lord. If the land of a liegeman is unjustly seized by his lord, he shall not be able to lodge a complaint against his lord if a year has not passed, and if he lodges the complaint before a year and a day have passed, he loses the fief. But a man of simple homage can lodge a complaint once forty days have passed. A liege noble has a Court while a man of simple homage cannot hold one.

73

What a husband gives his wife or what a wife gives her husband after they have been affianced, if it is feudal property, has no value whatsoever. However, one can give the other bourgeois goods, movable or immovable.

74

If the husband of a woman dies and there arises between the wife and the children or between others a dispute over the vassals owing homage or over the vassals of the latter, neither the vassals nor an individual vassal incur any prejudice by failing to render homage, until the aforementioned dispute is settled among the disputants.

75

Homage must be done by him who takes a wife who has a fief in the following way, to wit: first the wife shall do homage if she has not done so before; but if she has done homage, she is under no obligation, but the husband alone must perform it. And she must at once present her husband to her lord as a guardian, and thereupon he shall do homage, in accordance with what the land requires. Husband and wife shall render homage after their marriage has been solemnized.

76

A wife cannot, in truth, grant any part of her feudal dower except for her life, because the heir can revoke it, save if he himself has consented to the grant. What shall happen if the husband grants something from the dower of his wife? But if he should die and his widow should marry another, shall not the second husband be able to revoke that grant? You may say that, since the second is a guardian just like the first, he shall not be able to revoke it.

77

If a grant of a feudal holding has been made to someone by one who has the power to grant but who has not while still living placed the beneficiary in possession, after the death of the grantor the heir or the successor shall be able, if he wishes, to revoke the grant.

78

If a woman who is a free vassal has married a serf, during her married life she becomes the serf of her husband's lord and does not receive the produce of her fief. But after the death of her husband, she returns to her free status and recovers her fief; and her sons by the serf do not succeed to this fief. However, if she subsequently marries a freeman and has sons by him, these sons succeed to the fief.

79

A vassal—Prince or baron or female vassal—cannot invest any of his vassals if first he has not himself been invested by his suzerain; and the sub-vassal is not obliged to do him homage before the vassal has been invested. And if the vassal grants a feudal holding before being invested, though he has had seizin of that land or of part thereof, the grant is not valid.

80

A liegeman or liegewoman can, without asking the lord, marry his or her daughter to anyone that either may wish, even to a man of simple homage, provided that, above all, the land does not suffer any diminution on such an occasion.

81

If a vassal who is infirm makes a grant of land during his illness and later dies of this illness, the grant thus made has no validity. But if a grant is made before the illness and he is of sound mind, and if after taking ill he makes a privilege [confirming the grant], this privilege shall be valid and shall be sound and approved.

82

A vassal can commend his land to his lord and go outside of the Principality; this does not prejudice him except after two years and two days have elapsed, if he is bound to do personal service. But if he is not held to personal service, it is within his discretion to remain outside of the Principality as long as it pleases him, while supplying the service to which he is held. But if his lord dies, he is obliged to return in due time in order to do homage to the heir; and the due time is two years and two days. But when does the time begin to elapse, from the day of the vassal's departure or from that of the death of his lord? The answer is that it begins from the day of the lord's death.

83

Every guardian, whoever he may be, whether the Prince or another, ought to receive for the service which he owes to the lord of the fief the produce and the revenues of the fief which he holds in wardship, and he is obliged to provide sustenance and clothing for the ward whose guardian he is, and to rule the land. And if he accepts something illegally, beyond the expenses necessitated either by the service to his lord or by his administration of the affairs of the ward, he is obliged to return it to him whose guardian he is. Indeed, if the ward suffers any damage in his land through fraud, deceit, or negligence on the part of the guardian, the latter is bound to make reparations.

84

The rivers and streams which are found flowing through certain fiefs, or the sea along the shores of fiefs, belong to the said fiefs unless the lord has reserved them in the letters of his grant. Further, the lords of the said fiefs shall not be able to levy any duties when establishing a port or salt-works in them, without the permission of the Prince or of him who has rights over these fiefs.

85

When a ward has reached the age of fourteen, he can request the investiture of his fief, and his lord is obliged to invest him with the fief at once; but he is not bound to give him seizin or the produce of the fief until he has reached his fifteenth year. As for a girl, she is to request investiture when she enters upon her twelfth year, but her lord is not bound to grant her seizin or the produce of the fief until her twelve years are completed.

86

If a father or mother has sons or daughters, and these have begotten sons while the grandparents are still living, and if it happens that a son or daughter should die before the father or the mother, not having been invested with the paternal or maternal fiefs, after the death of the grandfather or grandmother, the grandsons or granddaughters shall have no part of the feudal land until they reach legal age.

87

If a lord should not wish to grant [the right of] *stivoria* [1] to his vassal, as he or his successor is obliged to, the vassal is not bound to give him any service. And if the vassal should wish to resign his fief to his lord, the produce gathered or found in the feudal land, as well as the produce which is yet to be gathered, belongs to him, in accordance with what has been ordered above respecting a deceased vassal.

[1] *Stivoria* meant some kind of customs or toll, the right to collect which was granted as a money fief in return for stipulated service. (The second sentence of this article, which seems to have no connection with the first, may be compared with the opening statement of art. 37.)

88

If a liegeman has been injured in his fief or a part thereof by the Prince or by another lord, the said liegeman is bound to request his lord thrice in a year before some of his liegemen that he restore to him that in which he aggrieved him or reinstate him in his fief, demanding the judgment of his court. Moreover, he is not obliged to render service until he has been reinstated in his fief. And, if the lord is not willing to do him full justice, in this case he [the vassal] must summon his peers and together with them summon his lord also. And if the lord is negligent in doing what justice requires, in this case the other lieges who are with him are not bound to serve their lord until the fief in question is reinstated.

89

If a vassal has reached the age of sixty, he is not obliged to serve his lord in person, but his son shall serve; and if he has no son, he must supply a knight if the fief is a knight's fief, or two squires if he cannot furnish a knight, until such time as he can furnish one. And if the fief is a sergeanty, he shall supply one squire.

90

If land has been granted to someone, and he has no letters of concession but has witnesses worthy of faith, the grant shall be valid for the lifetime of the recipient. And if the service is proved by the witnesses, the grant shall be valid for him and for the legitimate heirs of his body. But a grant so made shall not be valid for all heirs—even if the grantor held from the conquest—if there are no letters of donation. But what shall happen if the witnesses were not present when the service was imposed and it is proved that the vassal has rendered service for fifty or sixty years?

91

If a case arises that someone loses the letters [of concession] of his fief and can legitimately prove through witnesses that his house was burned or robbed and that he had and continues to have possession of his fief, reliance shall be placed on his oath concerning the loss of his letters. But if, in truth, one cannot prove the service, the service shall be imposed upon him by his lord and his lieges according to the nature of the fief. Moreover, the ancient register is proof sufficient.

92

If someone has the guardianship of a ward, and the lord by any means possible wishes to have the service of the fief, it shall be at the will of the guardian either to keep the fief or to give up the wardship. And if he gives it up, and later the fief becomes vacant, the guardian shall inherit, notwithstanding that he has renounced the wardship, because the wardship is distinct from the succession.

93

When a fief is granted to a husband and wife conjointly, if one dies before the other, the one surviving shall be lord; and, after his death, his son shall be [lord]. But if it is to two brothers or to others that the aforesaid grant is made, each person shall have his part; and if the one dies without sons, the other succeeds to the entire inheritance.

94

How No Person Can Construct a Castle in the Principality Without the Permission of the Prince.

No baron or vassal, whoever he may be, can construct a castle in the Principality of Achaia without the permission of the Prince, save if he is the lord or baron of land or of the twelve baronies whose lords have the right and just authority to construct a castle or castles in their own land. By the phrase "barons of land" is meant those who have blood-justice and a bishopric in their land. But cannot the other barons build castles? The answer is no.[1]

[1] Blood-justice, i.e., justice over life and limb, was the essential attribute of feudal high justice, and was often symbolized by the presence of a gallows.

95

How Land Cannot be Given to All of the Heirs.

A liege, whoever he may be, or a baron cannot grant land to all of the heirs unless he holds the land "for all heirs," for it is only according to the tenure by which one holds land that he can grant it. But how must the phrase "to all heirs of the grantee" be understood? The answer is: When this is expressed in the letters of concession, or when [the land] dates from the conquest of the Principality.

96

How No Person Can Grant Feudal Land to the Church, or to a Commune, or to a Serf Without the Permission of the Prince.

According to the Usage of the Empire of Romania, no vassal, whoever he may be, or baron can grant feudal land without the permission of the Prince to the Church, to any commune, or to a serf. But if he does make a grant, shall not the donation be valid during the life of the grantor? The answer is yes.

97

How the Wife of a Traitor Does Not Lose Her Dot or Her Dower Unless She Has Been Guilty.

The wife of a traitor does not lose her dot or her dower. She cannot, it is true, during her marriage request anything; but, after the death of her husband, she shall justly ask for her dot, unless she has been an accomplice in the treason.[1]

98

How It Is Sufficient for Those Who Hold a Fief Dating from the Conquest to Show the Ancient Seizin.

For those who hold a fief or fiefs dating from the conquest of the

[1] In all likelihood the customary feudal dower of one-half of the husband's lands is in question here, despite the use of both "dot" and "dower," between which we have distinguished in the Commentary.

Principality, it shall be enough if they show the ancient seizin. And if a landed holding is granted to someone for life, his wife shall not have a dower from this land. But what shall happen if the land has been granted to someone for the lifetime of the donor? Shall not the wife of the grantee, after the death of her husband, have a dower out of that land during the lifetime of the donor? The answer, according to some, is that of all the land which the husband of the woman possessed, she shall have half. And they even say that after the husband has peacefully held a landed holding during his life, his wife shall, following his death, have her dower, even if it is subsequently found that the husband held the land without just title: and this does not seem to be fair.

99

HOW A VASSAL IS BOUND TO AID THE LORD TO WHOM HE TOOK AN OATH IN THE FIRST INSTANCE.

A vassal who has several lords is obliged, if a war arises among them, to aid the one to whom he had first to take an oath and render homage.

100

WHEN SOMEONE HAPPENS TO BE OUTSIDE OF THE COUNTRY AND A FIEF BECOMES VACANT, WHO IS TO SUCCEED?

If a man or woman leaves the country with the consent of the lord, and if a fief to which one or the other is to succeed becomes vacant after his or her departure, if either does not appear within two years and two days, the nearest one in point of succession shall inherit and shall present himself within the specified period of time after the death of the lord of the fief. Be it clearly understood: if he who ought to inherit is outside of the Principality. Of course, if he is in the Principality, he is limited to a year and a day, and no hindrance can excuse him for being absent. But if the lord is to succeed, he can extend the limits indefinitely to suit his will.

101

How the Lord Can Grant One Who Is Outside of the Principality as Much Time as He Pleases.

When anyone leaves the Principality with the consent of his lord—the Prince or another lord—the lord can grant him as much time as he pleases while he is living. But if the lord dies, the vassal is obliged to return within the stipulated period in order to do homage to the successor of his lord or to his heir.

102

How the Grant of Feudal Land Is Valid for the Lifetime of the Grantor.

If a liegeman has granted a feudal holding for a service smaller than that attached to the land, the grant shall be valid for the lifetime of the grantor. And it is true that after the death of the grantor his heir shall prescribe the service required of that land.

103

How a Ward, After He Has Been Invested with His Land, Can Grant His Movable Goods.

A vassal under age, whoever he may be, after having been invested with his land, can grant his movable goods and make binding engagements and sell his belongings and purchase other goods and act in these matters just as if he had completed twenty-five years. But he cannot in truth make a grant of his fief if he has not first obtained the seizin of his land from his lord. And if he has been under the wardship of anyone, even if he has attained his majority of fifteen years, he cannot make any grant of his feudal land so long as the wardship lasts. And if a grant is made it shall be of no validity. The movable goods, it is true, he can grant.

104

How the Liegemen of One Lord Become the Lieges of Another.

When it happens that a vassal who has liegemen under him, even if it is the Prince, dies without leaving heirs of his body, the liegemen of this vassal become the lieges of the lord to whom the fief or the fiefs revert. And the said liegemen shall enjoy the liberty which they enjoyed while the first lord was alive.

105

How, if at the Order of the Church a Marriage Is Contracted Between Two Vassals Who Before the Said Marriage Had Sons, the Sons Can Succeed to the Fief.

If a vassal of single status has had intercourse with an unmarried woman and has had sons by her and later contracts marriage with her at the order of the Church, their sons are to succeed to the paternal or maternal fief. But if the vassal marries while he is suffering from disease, of which he dies, the sons shall not be held legitimate with respect to the succession of the fief, but [shall be so regarded] with respect to the movable goods. Nor should such a wife have a dower from the land of her husband, as I heard happened in the case of the wife and sons of Sire Guido Lombardo.

106

How the Land of a Vassal Who Has Been Captured by Enemies Shall Be Governed.

If a vassal is captured by enemies and has no wife but has sons of minor age, his land shall be governed by his procurator. And if he does not have a procurator or cannot appoint one while in prison, his lord shall appoint a procurator who shall govern the movable goods and the land for the sons and for the prisoner. Of course, if the vassal has a wife or sons of legal age or daughters, this wife or these sons shall govern the land. But the lord shall not be able to demand service of the procurator because the vassal was taken prisoner while in the service of his lord.

107

HOW A LIEGEMAN CAN GIVE A PERSON ONE OR TWO SERFS FOR A RETURN.

A liegeman can give one or two serfs or more to a person for some return, provided that he does not exceed the value of a fifth part of his fief or fiefs. And such a vassal is not obliged to take an oath of fealty or homage, but the investiture of his lord is sufficient.

108

HOW THE SONS OF A VASSAL AND HIS WIFE, ORPHANED WHILE MINORS, OUGHT TO RECEIVE SUSTENANCE AND DRESS FROM THE PATERNAL GUARDIAN.

If two vassals enter into matrimony and later have sons and daughters, and if these sons and daughters are orphaned of both their father and mother while still minors, they shall receive food and raiment from the guardian of the fief of the father and mother. And in truth, after the eldest son or eldest daughter has reached legal age and has obtained the seizin of the land of the father or mother, he is bound to give food and raiment to his brothers and his sisters as long as they choose to live with him.

109

HOW THE ELDEST DAUGHTER, HAVING A BROTHER YOUNGER THAN HERSELF, AFTER THE DEATH OF HER FATHER, ON ARRIVING AT HER MAJORITY, SHOULD BE INVESTED AND SHALL REMAIN IN POSSESSION UNTIL HER BROTHER REACHES LEGAL AGE.

If a vassal or his wife dies leaving a son or daughter of minor age, the eldest daughter, after she has attained legal age, should be invested with the paternal or maternal fief and shall possess the land until the male child shall reach legal age.

110

How the Land Remains to the Wife When, Her Husband Having Died, She Is Left with Child.

If a female vassal is found to be with child at the time that her husband dies, the land of her husband remains to her, notwithstanding that neither a son nor a daughter results from the union, unless, after becoming pregnant, she indulges in lascivious conduct.

111

How in Three Instances a Lord Cannot Deny Permission to His Vassal to Go Outside of the Principality.

In three cases, the Prince or another lord cannot deny permission to his vassal to leave the Principality: namely, if a succession falls vacant to him outside of the Principality; if he wishes to depart in order to contract a marriage; or if he desires to go to the Holy Sepulcher, or to Rome to the Apostles Saint Peter and Saint Paul, or to Saint James [of Compostella]. And he is limited to two years and two days, else he loses his fief. But in this case is a judgment necessary or not? Or can a hindrance excuse him?

112

When a Feudal Holding May Be Granted by Someone Who Has the Power to Do So.

When a feudal holding has been granted to someone by the Prince or by another lord who has the right to grant land, and it is stipulated in the donation that after the death of the grantee his wife should not get half of that land but that it should pass to the heirs of the grantee, the wife shall nevertheless have half of the land notwithstanding the stipulation placed in the donation.

113

How a Widowed Woman Is Not Burdened with Any Service for Forty Days.

In order that widowed vassals may not be burdened with feudal service, it was ordered that after the death of their husbands they should not for forty days be obliged to perform any service to which they are bound by reason of the fief or fiefs which they hold from their lords.

114

When Someone Leaves Something to a Female Vassal Who Has Married.

If somebody bequeaths to a female vassal who has a husband some money or objects and adds that this money or these things should not pass into the hands of the husband, they shall pass to the husband if they pass into the hands of the wife while the husband is living. And the reason is namely this: that from the moment that the goods are in the wife's control, that is, in her hands, they belong to the husband, except if they have not come into her hands while the husband was living, since after the husband's death the said goods shall remain to the wife.

115

How He Who Has Several Fiefs Can Renounce One of Them.

If somebody has several fiefs, acquired together or one after the other, he can, if he desires, renounce some of them and retain the others. And if he has performed the service fixed for some of them, these must not be seized for others, for which he is not performing the prescribed service.

116

How a Lord Is Not Bound to Put Someone in Possession of a Fief When It Is Vacant, and Several Ask for It, Until Such Time as a Judgment of the Court Has Been Declared.

When a fief becomes vacant through the death of a vassal, and several persons present themselves, each of them claiming to be the nearest relative in the succession of the said fief, the lord of whom the fief is held can and must invest the claimants with the fief while reserving his right and that of everyone else. And he is not bound to place somebody in possession of the fief until it has been set forth by judgment of his Court who is the nearest relative in the matter of acquiring the fief. But what shall happen if nobody presents himself for forty days and it is moreover plain that the heir is in the Principality? Shall the lord be able to seize that land? I believe that he shall be able to, on account of the negligence of the heir. I further believe that he can do so at once on account of this negligence.

117

That No Official Can Seize the Land of a Vassal.

In the Usages of the Empire of Romania this was decreed, namely, that no official of the Prince can seize the land of any vassal except only the bailiff or the captain appointed to the command by the said Prince, to which captain the vassals are held to pay the service owed and ordered.

118

How the Lord Can Seize the Land of a Vassal Who Dies Until an Heir Appears.

If a vassal, either male or female, dies outside of the Principality and no heir appears to present himself to the lord, the lord of whom the fief is held can seize the land of the deceased until the heir appears within the prescribed time. He cannot, it is true, seize the goods and produce of this land, movable or livestock, or the bourgeois goods of the deceased, but his procurator shall hold them until the lord has ascertained definitely whether the deceased died testate or intestate. And if he died intestate, the goods shall be kept for a year for the heir or for the nearest relative if he appears. Otherwise, they shall be distributed for the repose of the soul of the deceased, as is ordained above.

119

How a Female Vassal Can Arrange to Marry by Paying Relief.

If a female vassal holds in liege and simple homage of the same lord, she shall be able to marry freely whom she wishes by paying relief. And if she marries without paying relief, she incurs no penalty, but she is held to pay the relief. And if she holds in liege homage of one lord and in simple homage of another, in this case the lord of simple homage can order her not to marry except by his permission, if it will please him.

120

How a Vassal Must Present Himself to His Lord Within Forty Days and Request Investiture.

When a vassal presents himself within forty days to his lord of whom he is to hold the land, asking to be invested by him, and this lord does not wish to invest him, saying that he should protect him from every injury that he might incur, and if the lord has not imposed any fixed period on him, in this case the vassal shall have a year in which to ask for the investiture. But if the period is increased, in this case he shall be held to the limits which he was ordered to observe.

121

If a vassal dies leaving a wife and a son or a daughter, the wife succeeding to half of his land, even though the son or daughter may have neglected for a year to ask for the investiture of the land of the father, nevertheless, after the death of the mother, he can ask for the investiture of the land which the mother or stepmother possessed, in spite of his earlier negligence.[1]

122

When a person holds land of another for an annual rental, he is not required to take an oath to him when he is invested with this land. But he must request the investiture at the time required, like other vassals, and his lord must invest him with the hood. It is true, if this vassal has his casal in a city, a castle, or a villa of the Prince, or of another vassal, by reason of this tenement the superior lord shall be able to demand of this vassal an oath of fealty.

123

By the Custom of the Empire of Romania it is observed that a vassal obliged to perform an annual service—either personally or through a substitute—or some minor service, if he fails to fulfill this service, cannot be forced to perform it, once the year for doing so has passed; nor on this account can his land be seized. But [thereafter] he shall be required to perform the service to which he is bound, as if he had previously performed it.

124

It has been observed that, according to the Usage of the Empire of Romania, he who succeeds to someone's fief, whether a son, daughter or anyone else, is not obliged to pay the debts of his predecessor on account of the fief, since the fief is held to a stipulated service and not for any debt. But whoever shall receive the movable goods of the deceased is obliged to discharge the debts. And in the payments which are to be made to the creditors, the wife must be paid before all others in respect to her dot and any increase thereof.

[1] The "succession" of the wife to her husband's land is of course not a true instance of inheritance; she merely has a life usufruct in the half of the fief to which she is entitled as dower (see Commentary on the Feudal Dower).

125

If a female serf contracts marriage with a freeman, notwithstanding the opposition of the lord of the serf, this serf becomes free. And if the husband dies before his wife, she remains none the less free on that account.

126

If a liege vassal has feudal land in his own right and has a liege holding through his wife in different castellanies, and if he is bound to personal service for both the one and the other, he is obliged first of all to serve in the castellany where he has his own inheritance; and for his wife's land he shall provide the service through a substitute. It shall be the same if he has an inherited holding of his wife in one castellany and another holding for the dower of his wife in another castellany, since he shall give personal service for his wife's own land and the prescribed service for the dower land, provided that these castellanies belong to the same lord.

127

When the Prince or another baron or a liegeman makes a grant of feudal land to two persons, one after the other, that one shall be the principal holder in the land who on the command of the grantor shall have acquired the seizin of the land. But what shall happen if the grant has been made with the permission of the lord? The reply: it shall be valid.

128

No baron or other liegeman can grant feudal land or a serf except in exchange for service or for some recognition. And if he makes a grant without service or recognition, it shall have no validity; but this grantor shall not be able to revoke that grant during his life.

129

If a man who is not a liege contracts marriage with a woman of liege homage, he becomes a liege by virtue of the liege land of his wife, even if the wife holds that land in fief as her dower.

130

If a vassal who has two sisters dies without leaving heirs of his body, and the two sisters have sons, and if the first of the sisters dies before the said brother, the second sister shall succeed to half of the fief, as the closest relative, and the wife of the father [brother] to the other half. But if afterwards the sister who succeeds to the fief dies before the mother or the stepmother [that is, the widow], who has the other half of the fief by reason of her dower, the son of the second sister, who succeeds to half of the fief, ought to succeed to this inheritance, and not the son of the first sister. And the reason for this is that this half of the fief should return to the first heir who inherited.

131

When a vassal is the guardian of a minor, either a boy or a girl, and the land of the minor falls to the said guardian by inheritance, the guardian must appear before the lord, ask for the investiture and render the homage which this land requires, notwithstanding that he may have first done homage as guardian, since, in the present case, it is as the heir that he shall appear and shall render homage.

132

Similarly, it arises from the Usages of the Empire of Romania that the renunciation or acknowledgment which the wife makes to her husband of the dot she has received or of a loan made to her during her marriage is of no validity, even though an oath be taken in the matter.

133

By the Customs of the Empire of Romania it is set forth that a vassal in a state of illness from which he dies cannot bequeath or renounce his fief or a part thereof to the detriment of his heir; nor even, being in good health in his lifetime, if his predecessors have acquired the fief, can he renounce it. But if he has acquired a fief, it is true that he can renounce it, while in good health and even though it be to the prejudice of his heir, in the presence of the lord. But to bequeath the said fief he cannot, even to his lord, nor even the smallest part of that fief, if he does injury to his heir.

134

If a liegeman has given a fief to one who has a wife, or who does not have one, the grant to last as long as it pleases the will of the grantor, and if the grantee dies before the grantor changes his wish, his wife shall have a dower out of this grant following her husband's death.

135

When someone acquires a feudal holding in various castellanies belonging to one lord and afterwards one of these is given to another lord, the vassal must furnish the principal service there where he holds the greatest land. And for the other, smaller land, the service shall be imposed by the lord of that land, if the service does not appear diminished and is service according to [the revenues] to be derived from that land.

136

It is further contained in the Customs of the Empire that when a bailiff is sent to govern the said Empire or the said Principality on the part of the Emperor or of the Prince, in order that he may be received as bailiff by the subjects of these rulers, it is necessary that he take an oath with his hand on the Gospels that he shall observe, and to the full extent of his power shall cause to be observed by his officials, the franchises and usages of the Empire of Romania, that is, the Empire of Constantinople.

137

How It Is Enough for a Widowed Vassal to Prove Only That Her Husband Possessed This Land Without Opposition and in Quiet Enjoyment.

In order that a widowed vassal may obtain for her dower half of the feudal land which her husband possessed at the time that their marriage was solemnized, it is necessary and it shall suffice that she prove only that her husband had possession of this land at the aforesaid time in quiet enjoyment and without opposition. But the heir who succeeds to this land is obliged to show his lord how he holds the land of him. It is true that if the lord of the vassal succeeds to this land, the vassal's widow is not obliged to prove other than what is contained above.

138

How the Sons or Daughters of Greek Vassals Inherit Fiefs Equally.

To the fiefs of Greek vassals which have been held from an early date their sons or their daughters shall succeed equally. But if the fief belongs to a Greek female vassal and she marries a Latin and sons or daughters are born to them, after the death of the mother it shall be the same for the sons born to them: they shall succeed equally when they arrive at the lawful age notwithstanding that their father was a Frank. And in the request for investiture no prejudice shall result from the period of forty days or of a year to those who hold fiefs according to the manner of the Greeks. Others say the contrary with more verisimilitude, unless the [Greek] vassals are serfs.

139

How a Grant Made to a Serf, if It Is a Written Transaction, Is Valid for the Lifetime of the Grantor.

If a Frankish vassal has granted liberty to his serf and has given him a feudal holding after his liberation, the grant is valid during the life of him who made and granted it provided that there appear the letters of the enfranchisement; otherwise he himself can revoke the aforesaid acts.

140

How a Liegeman or Liegewoman Is Not Obliged to Make a Payment for the Houses Which He Inhabits.

A liegeman or liegewoman is not obliged to make a payment for the houses which he inhabits or to supply a guard in the land where the houses are situated. But if either has other houses, or vineyards, he is bound to supply the aforesaid things.

141

How the Wife of a Vassal, if Her Husband Has Given Up His Fief to His Lord, Is Not to Have a Dower out of What Her Husband Has Renounced.

If a vassal contracts marriage with a woman and gives up into his lord's hands the fief which he holds of him, to whom he can renounce it, after his death his wife shall not obtain anything for her dower from the fief renounced by her husband. But if the husband acquires feudal land during the marriage, shall he be able to give up this land to the prejudice of his wife? The answer is no.

142

If a Lord Has Granted Somebody a Vineyard or a Bourgeois Field.

If the Prince or another lord has given a vineyard or a bourgeois field to someone and to the heirs descended of his body for an annual rent, and if he to whom it was given dies, having had no heirs of his body, the grantor shall succeed to the things given. But if mention was made in the letter that he was giving him this thing in burgessy, in this case he to whom it was given can, if he wishes, sell that object and bequeath it to whom it pleases him. And if he dies intestate, the nearest relative succeeds as if the object were movable goods. And the Prince can make a bourgeois tenement of the fief or of part thereof.

143

How One Can Appeal from the Inferior Court to the Superior Court.

By the Custom of the Empire of Romania there is an appeal from the inferior court of any baron, liegeman, vassal, or official of the Prince to the principal court if the Prince is present . . . .[1] his lord, the other from degree to degree; and from the bailiff of the Principality of Achaia to the Prince, if he is present in the Principality; and from the Prince to the Emperor when one has been wronged; and while the appeal is pending, no changes can be made. Further, in cases concerning money or debts, there is no appeal from a judgment to the High Court of the Prince. Excepting this: that if one has seized a fief of the vassal of his liegeman, even unjustly, the sub-vassal cannot have recourse to his superior lord except at the end of a year and a day and unless the terms set forth above have been respected.

144

How One Must Proceed When a Judgment Is Made and in What Conditions a Judgment Is Valid or No.

If the High Court or another court proceeds to a judgment after the sun has set, this judgment is not valid. And if such procedure occurs on a feast day, the judgment is valid. But in truth, if one party objects that he does not wish that the court proceed to a judgment on a feast day, the lord must postpone the proceedings. And no one can litigate in a feudal matter through a procurator, save if the opposing party consents to it. Furthermore, when sentence is to be announced, the chief parties must be present.

145

How in a Court No Memorandum Can Be Presented, nor Is an Advocate Accepted Who Speaks by Reading.

In the High Court and in the other, inferior courts, a *libellus* cannot be presented, but a petition can quite properly be offered.

[1] There is a lacuna at this point in the manuscripts.

Nor is an advocate accepted who speaks from script or cites the laws or canons, but one must propound and defend the case of his party in the vulgar tongue; and this is fitting, inasmuch as the liegemen, for the greater part, are unlettered men. Verily, when a question cannot be decided by the Usages of the said Empire, in that case the lord and the members of his court can have recourse, in order to receive counsel, to whomever it will please them.[1]

146

When Two Legal Disputants Ask That Counsel Be Given Them, What Should Be Done?

When two parties engage in litigation and one of them, or the one and the other, asks that counsel be given them by the lord, the lord is bound to give them as their counsel some one or more of his liegemen, while retaining for himself those whom he wishes as his own counsel. But he is not bound to provide an advocate. And subsequently, these counselors who shall be given to the party, once their conclusions have been made, shall be able to take part in the judgment mentioned. However, if he who has brought the suit is a person of wretched station without the wherewithal to pay someone to present and plead his case, the lord is held to provide him with someone to present his case and defend it for him.

147

How There Is No Right of Prescription Between a Lord and His Vassal.

Between a lord and his vassal there is reciprocally no right of prescription. Nor between the Church and a vassal, and conversely, does prescription run in [questions of] immovable goods or of serfs? But what about movable goods and livestock?

[1] In canonical and Roman civil procedure the *libellus* was a short written statement of his claim presented by the plaintiff to begin an action; it was drawn up by an advocate. Procedure in feudal trials was entirely oral. We may assume that the "petition" here was the spoken statement of the plaintiff.

148

How if Someone Is Cited in a Civil or Pecuniary Case and Fails to Appear at the Third Citation, Sentence Shall Be Reached.

When a vassal, or whoever he may be, is cited in a civil case that is not feudal, or in a pecuniary case, on the petition of anyone else, if he is cited three times and is contumacious, the court shall hear the testimony. And if the plaintiff proves his charges, the court shall proceed to a final sentence, no longer summoning him who has been contumacious.

149

How There Is No Need of a Notary Public in Order to Make a Will.

When a testament is to be made, it is not necessary that a notary public be present, but it is sufficient if two or three witnesses—liegemen or other—are together with the testator, provided that they are deserving of trust and that they place their seals of wax upon the will. And if by chance on this occasion someone has no seal, in such a case it is sufficient if the wish of the testator is proved by testimonials, that is, that the witnesses are freemen, that is, non-servile. But, in this case, could one prove good faith by serfs or not? And if the will is charged with being false, such a question shall be decided before the secular court. And if the question arises whether the will is valid or not, to ascertain this is the task of an ecclesiastical judge. But to whom should cases respecting bequests for pious foundations be referred if the heir or the executor does not wish to pay them? The answer is: before the diocesan. But as for other bequests, to whom should they be referred?

150

How Documents Should Be Corroborated by Seals.

A document that is drawn up in the Principality, if it is not corroborated by the seals of the witnesses, is of no validity. It is true, if it is drawn up outside of the Principality, that it is valid and enforceable.

151

IF A LIEGEMAN KILLS A SERF, WHAT SHOULD BE DONE?

If it happens that a liegeman should kill a serf by misadventure, he is required to give the latter's lord another serf worth as much as the victim. But if he acted on premeditation, he shall submit to the sentence of the liegemen of the lord at the place where the homicide was committed, if the lord of the place has jurisdiction in criminal matters.

152

HOW ALL FREEMEN CAN SELL THEIR REVENUES WITHOUT *COMMERCIUM*.

All the vassals and other freemen of the aforementioned Principality can freely sell their produce, revenues, or profits without *commercium*, both in the Principality and to others who wish to buy them and take them outside of the Principality, unless these are enemies.[1] An exception is made when, on account of the needs of the country and through the Prince with the counsel and consent of his lieges, it may be ordered that during a certain period no property can be taken outside of the Principality.

153

HOW, IF THERE IS LITIGATION FOR A VACANT FIEF, THAT FIEF SHOULD BE SEQUESTERED.

If it happens that a fief or part of a fief becomes vacant and a dispute arises between two persons, in this case it is just that the

[1] *Commercium* refers to customs duties, as we know from several documents pertaining to Morea. One of these is a charter of Philip of Savoy and Princess Isabella of 1303, by which they granted a money-fief of 300 hyperpers a year to Jacquemin de Scalenges against the receipts of the port of Glarentza (*sour nostre comercle de Clarence*), in return for personal service of three months a year. (Buchon, *Recherches historiques sur la principauté française de Morée* [2 vols., Paris, 1845], II, 383–84.)

fief or the part thereof be sequestered by the lord and handed over to someone worthy of trust until the aforementioned dispute is settled. But what shall happen if the dispute is between the lord and those who ask for the fief? The answer is that the fief shall remain in the hands of the lord while the dispute is being adjudged.

154

How the Husband Must Pay the Debts of His Wife.

The husband must pay the debts of his wife even though his wife incurred the debts before the marriage between them was contracted, if from her he has received movable goods or livestock, even if his wife is dead. And if the wife is living, the husband is obliged to pay the debts, even if he has not received any movable goods from his wife.

155

When a Treasure Is Found, or Has Been Found, What Must Be Done?

When a treasure is found in some place by a freeman and on his own land, he who finds it gets half of it and the Prince the other half. And if he finds it in the land of another, the lord gets the third part of it—that is, he who is lord of the fief or of the bourgeois land—the finder receives a third, and the Prince the remaining third. And if the finder is a serf, the right of the serf passes to his lord.

156

How a Married Woman Cannot Dispose of Her Dot by Will.

A married woman cannot dispose of her dot by will, since her husband obtains the dot,[1] nor yet of her movable or immovable goods outside of her dot, without the permission of her husband, because that which the wife acquires during the marriage by succession to a legacy or by donation belongs to the husband, un-

[1] While the husband has control of the dot during the marriage, unless a living child has resulted from the marriage he does not get possession of the dot after his wife's death (rather her family does); cf. art. 174 and Commentary on Dot.

less agreements or conventions to the contrary exist. And if a liegeman or any other freeman takes to wife a woman who has bourgeois goods, everything goes to the husband; and the sons of a first marriage do not inherit anything. And it is the same if a liegewoman or vassal has bourgeois or movable goods and one who does not hold of liege homage takes her to wife; this property goes to the husband unless agreements to the contrary exist or the wife survives the husband, living after him; for in this case the bourgeois goods remain to her. But the movable property may not remain to her if the husband has left a will.[2]

157

WHEN ONE WISHES TO DO BATTLE WITH ANOTHER, HE MUST GIVE THE WAGER OF BATTLE.

If somebody wishes to do battle with another person, according to the Custom of the Empire of Romania, he can do so by giving the wager of battle.

158

HOW IT IS ENOUGH TO PROVE BY LIEGEMEN THAT A SENTENCE HAS BEEN GIVEN, EVEN IF THE SENTENCE IS NOT FOUND.

If judgment has been passed on someone and the sentence does not appear in writing, it shall be enough if the said judgment is attested by two or more liegemen who participated in it. But what is to be done if not liegemen but other men worthy of faith could attest the said matter?

[2] Arts. 37 and 142 clearly affirm that a man can will his bourgeois holdings, immovable and movable. Here we read that a wife succeeds to bourgeois goods, because, it is implied, the husband could not hold such goods. What appears to be a contradiction may simply be due to careless phrasing in the original: the surviving wife keeps the bourgeois goods *because* of a marriage agreement, not because she simply survived or because the husband cannot in any case dispose of bourgeois goods.

159

How Pastures and Hunting Lands of the Subjects of the Prince Are Common.

Just as the pastures and hunting preserves of the subjects of the Prince are common according to the Usages of the Empire of Romania, similarly it was decreed that the pastures and hunting lands of the Prince shall be common among him and his liegemen. But what of the other vassals? Moreover, if a meadow has been declared reserved for the lord or his subject, for their horses, it shall belong to the lord of the field. In the forests, in truth, which have been anciently reserved and which are set aside to supply the castles, no one can take anything from them unless he is lord of the forest. In truth, inhabitants of the great forests can cut wood from trees which bear no fruit, in order to build their houses and for their needs; and the other neighbors can cut dry wood, that is, from trees which bear no fruit. The serfs who live in the great forests can put out their swine to eat the acorns which lie on the ground and pasture them. Of a certainty, the wild forest is common to all.

160

How There Must Be Granted a Delay of Fifteen Days to One Who Holds a Fief or Part of a Fief When He Is Presented with a Lawsuit; and Afterwards Still Further Delays.

When someone brings a suit against somebody who possesses a fief or part of a fief, the one in possession shall be given a delay of fifteen days in order to take counsel with himself, if he asks for the time; and then he shall have another fifteen days in which to ask and look for counsel; and later, fifteen more days in which to make reply. And if he is contumacious after the said fifteen days have passed, in that case the Court shall place his opponent in possession of the object demanded. But if he fails to appear after the first citation, what shall happen? The answer is that he must be cited three times, and if at the third summons he does not appear and remains contumacious, his opponent shall be placed in possession of the object demanded. But if he does appear, he shall have a period of forty days for his defense. And if within the said forty days, detained by a just hindrance, he cannot lawfully defend himself, he shall have still another forty days. Finally, the Court has forty days to decide the case. And the same period is designated to prove how someone holds feudal land from his lord. But what is to be done if he who brings a citation against another shall himself be contumacious by failing to appear? The answer is that he shall pay the expenses of him who was cited, and the plaintiff shall recommence the suit anew. If the point at issue is not decided by witnesses, some people may advise the defendant that he should say nothing in his defense until the period stated above; and in such a case he should ask what follows, which I do not recommend. But it is a safer way to say something while making known by protest that one still intends to produce his defense in the period which will follow.

161

How in Killing Someone in Self-Defense, One Does Not Merit a Penalty.

The vassal, or whoever it may be, [who] in defending himself will kill someone, does not for this merit any penalty.

162

How One Cannot Enter the Casal of a Vassal Without His Permission.

The official of the Prince, or of whomever you will, cannot nor ought to enter the casal of a vassal in order to buy something there against the will of the lord of the casal. And the reason is that, after he has performed the service, the lord need not trouble himself about the serfs of his vassal except if there is a criminal case.

163

How a Party to a Lawsuit Can Challenge the Counsel of His Lord on Grounds of Suspicion.

If a party to a lawsuit has any suspicion regarding the counsel of his lord, he can challenge him to the judgment if he proves the legitimate cause of his suspicion.

164

How One Cannot Call Others Traitors nor Swear Falsely.

If a vassal or others, whoever they may be, call another person a traitor before the Court, and they cannot prove the charge, they are held to the penalty that the one accused should have borne. And if someone while taking oath in a matter of testimony should bear false witness, he must not again be taken as witness in any case; and he must, moreover, pay seventy-two hyperpers; [1] otherwise he loses his hand.

165

Concerning Booty Gained Through Force of Arms.

If men of feudal arms performing their service go against the enemy and gain some booty, and if the captain of the Prince has been present, the lord [Prince] shall have half of the booty and the other half shall be apportioned according to the rank of the men of arms. And if the captain has not been present, the booty is to go to those who shall win it. But in truth, if by [public] clamor some men go out against the enemy and booty is thus recovered from the enemy on the same day [on which it was taken by the enemy], the booty shall be restored to its proper lord or lords. But if the booty remains in the hands of the enemy for a day and a

[1] The hyperper was a gold coin of Constantinople which the Franks also called bezant (from Byzantium). As it lost its value under the Palaiologi (1261–1453), the Venetian gold ducat replaced it as the monetary standard in the East. The hyperper is generally considered to have been worth about half a pound, or $2.50.

night, it shall be conceded to those who shall win it, in accordance with the description given above.

166

If somebody should say to another: I command thee under penalty of one hundred hyperpers to do such and such a thing or not to do it, he to whom the command is given is not obliged to obey it, unless he who gives the command has power or jurisdiction over him.

167

When a person deserts his lord in battle and flees before the battle has been lost, he deserves to be disinherited of his land by judgment of the court of his lord. And if a man kills another man and is taken, and is punished with death by the court, he does not lose his [movable] goods but can freely dispose of his goods by will, unless he is a traitor.

168

A party, if he so wishes, can request that a sentence of judgment be given in written form. And the court is bound to give it to him under the seals of those who make the judgment. And the lord is bound to have the judgment of his court placed in writing in his register.

169

If a person lays violent hands upon an official of his lord while not acting in self-defense, he shall be subject to the judgment of the liegemen of his lord, that they may impose the penalty on him. But what shall this penalty be? In reply I believe [it should be] arbitrary, inasmuch as it is not determined. By officials are meant the Protovestiary and the Treasurer of the Prince, and the Captain of Arms.[1] But what happens if a castellan or boon companion of the Prince is involved?

[1] For the character of these officials see the Commentary, "The Feudal Hierarchy and the Grand Officers."

170

In order that a contract may be legal, adhered to and valid by the fact of its having been made according to the Usages of the Empire of Constantinople, it is sufficient if it is stated in the letters or documents that the parties renounce all the Usages of the Empire of Constantinople and the exceptions introduced by them, and it is not necessary that the laws or canons be renounced.

171

If some of the revenues of the Prince which it is customary for his officials (who are so commanded) to sell at certain periods are sold before the customary periods, unless the consent of the Prince or of his lieutenant has followed it, the sale shall not be valid. You ought to know that by the Usage of the Principality it is established that to the Protovestiary belongs the sale of the revenues of the Prince, and to the Treasurer belong the collection and distribution of the monies.

172

If a thing is sold at less than half of the just price or if it is let out at hire, the buyer or renter must make up what is lacking in the price, or else the money he has given shall be returned to him, save if the seller or lessor ignores this exception introduced by him or if the said object is sold or rented at auction, because in this case the sale or the renting shall remain fixed and approved.

173

If one to whom a grant of land has been made acquires possession of that land through his own authority, such possession is not valid because the grantor must give somebody his power so that with this authority he can place the grantee in possession. It is true, if the latter shows his privilege and proves his possession, that shall suffice.

174

If a serf marries the serf of another lord, his wife becomes the serf of her husband's lord, even after the death of her husband, so long as children—and these may have died immediately—have been born to the couple. And if the wife dies before her husband, he obtains the dot. However, if the wife dies without having had children, the dot reverts to the father or mother or to the brothers in the following manner, to wit: the goods that appear, whether they are movable or livestock, or whether it is proved that these goods were sold and from the money other property was bought, can be demanded in the name of the dot. The food that is in the house, or seed, shall be divided by the family among the father, the sons and the others, by individual according to who shall be found in the house. Always excepting that if children had resulted from the marriage, even though they were not alive—provided only that they had uttered a cry, the husband obtains the dot. And if the wife has neither father, mother, nor brothers and has had no children, her lord succeeds. And a serf cannot marry his daughter or contract marriage himself without the permission of his lord. And if he has contracted marriage, the lord can punish him arbitrarily and seize the dot which his male or female serf has given: this, of course, if the dot is found in the domain of the lord of the female serf. Otherwise, if the female serf has brought the dot to the domain of her husband's lord, in this case the first lord cannot take anything, unless he had prohibited the serf [her father] from marrying his daughter or had forbidden the female serf from contracting marriage. But if the husband dies leaving heirs by this wife, she remains with her sons in the domain of her husband's lord. However, if the husband dies without heirs, his wife can, if she so wishes, return to her first lord. But she can in no way depart the place where she lived with her husband in order to give herself to a lord other than her first one. As for illegitimate sons, the offspring follow the status of the mother, even if the father had been free. In the case of legitimate sons, the offspring follow the status of the father.

175

How a Serf Cannot Give Testimony Concerning an Entire Fief.

A serf cannot give testimony in what concerns an entire fief, but he can do so regarding a part thereof, that is, concerning a vineyard, a piece of land, or a serf. Moreover, the limits of fields, of lands, of forests or of other things can be proved by the testimony of serfs. And in regard to testimony, more credence is given to outside serfs than to those of litigants.

176

What Happens When a Serf of a Fief Is Owned by Another Vassal?

If a lord has given a fief to someone and in another place there has been found a serf of the said fief in the possession of another vassal, the serf is obliged to return to the lord of the said fief, unless he remains under a prescriptive right of thirty [years]. Let it be clearly understood that prescription does not run between a lord and his vassal, reciprocally.

177

When the Serfs of Vassals Quarrel Among Themselves and One Strikes Another, What Should Be Done?

When two serfs of vassals quarrel together and one strikes the other, the penalty levied on the one who struck the blow is to be paid over to the lord, unless the accusation was first taken to the Court of the Prince by him who had sustained the injury, or to the court of him who has right and justice in that country, according to the Usage of the Empire of Romania; or unless the offense was committed in a place where the lord has a captain to dispense justice, like Glarentza or Androusa.

178

How a Grant Made to a Serf Is Valid During the Life of the Grantor.

A grant made by one who is able to do so of a piece of land to one of his own serfs or to an outside serf, that is, to a serf of another lord, is valid for the life of the grantor. But after his death his heir or successor can revoke the grant if he is pleased to do so. But if the grant is made to a Greek landowner, it cannot be revoked either by the heir or by the successor.

179

How the Sons Born to a Serf and a Female Serf Belonging to Different Lords Shall Remain Serfs of the Lord of the Female Serf.

If an unmarried serf of a vassal has relations with an unmarried serf of another lord and sons are born to them, although they might later marry, the children are no less the serfs of their mother's lord.

180

How the Sons of a Serf Who Has Married a Free Woman Become Serfs of Their Father's Lord

If a free woman who is not a vassal marries a serf, during the life of her husband she becomes the serf of his lord. And if she survives her husband, she returns to her pristine liberty while her children remain serfs. But what shall happen if she is a vassal? Her condition shall be the same.

181

How a Serf Who Shall Be Subject to Some Person Cannot Leave Without His Permission.

If a serf born outside of the Principality enters it and places himself under a freeman and the freeman owns him for a year and a day, or if he is a *nicario* born outside of the Principality who has paid the *nicariado* for the period stated above, should he wish to leave he cannot do so without the permission of him to whom he shall be subject or to whom he pays the *nicariado,* even if he wished to leave in order to establish himself in the demesne of the Prince, the reason being that he becomes the serf of the said freeman.[1]

182

How a Serf Who Has Remained on the Land of a Vassal for Thirty Years Becomes His Serf.

If a serf born in the Principality remains for thirty years on the land of another vassal, holding land or a vineyard from him or acknowledging him as a lord, and if the serf's own lord has not made any request of him, and the serf, moreover, makes no payment as a sign of subjection, the serf shall belong to him whose man he has been for thirty years. However, if he is a *nicario* and was born in the Principality, he is not prescribed by any period of time.

183

When a *Zurado* Is Given to the Church, What Occurs?

When a *zurado* is given to the Church by some vassal, the *zurado* along with his children and with the entire *staxia* remains to the Church. After the death of the father, the Church chooses one of the sons whom it desires with the entire *staxia,* and the others remain to the lord who granted the *zurado,* or to his heir. Furthermore, the *zurado* is required each year to give to the lord of the casal the *acrostico* or *chrustilio,* that is to say, wax, fowl, or eggs.[1]

[1] It is difficult to determine the exact status of a *nicario,* a type of serf mentioned again in arts. 182, 184, and 214. His status seems to have been still lower than that of the ordinary Moreot serf.

---

[1] A conditional grant of land to the Church is in question here. It is impossible to give precise definitions of *zurado* and *staxia. Staxia,* from its mention here and in arts. 190, 197, 205, and 215, as well as in other documents of the Latin domination in Greece, may have designated a peasant holding of more or less "standard" size and services. The regular services owed the lord were called *dispoticaria* (art. 190; from the Greek meaning "master" or "lord"). The *acrostico* or *crustilio* (also 190; from *akrostichon,* the Byzantine land tax) was a small payment in kind, a "recognitory" rent indicating the

184

What Should Happen When a Serf Has Planted a Vine on the Land of Another Vassal?

When the serf of a vassal has planted a vine on the land of another vassal with his permission, the serf has half of the vine if other agreements do not appear; and afterward, when the vine is destroyed, the land returns to the first lord of the land. And if he has left the place or has died without leaving children, his lord inherits—that is, if for this vineyard he has paid him something and the lord of the land has consented to this rental. However, if he is the *nicario* of somebody who owns a piece of land and has planted something in this land, and if he leaves this place or dies without issue, the lord of the land inherits all the things planted and buildings, whether or not the serf pays a rental for the land. But if he is not known and flees, or dies without issue, the inheritance goes to the lord of the casal of which the land at the beginning was a part.

185

How the Lord of a Serf Inherits His Goods if the Latter Dies Without Heirs.

If a serf of whatever lord dies without heirs of his body, the lord succeeds to his movable and immovable goods, even if he has made a will without his lord's permission.

---

lord's superior right in the land, not a true rent based on the land's income (cf. art. 128). It is comparable to the *cens* (cf. art. 192) which the free peasant paid. Peasant holdings were usually divided equally among the heirs, unlike noble fiefs. The prohibition stated in article 190 apparently applies to division among the father and sons while the parent was still living. *Zurado* may have been used only to designate the holder of a *staxia* granted to the Church on the conditions described in art. 183. The *acrostico* paid to the lord was a mere token; the Church got the full use of the *staxia*, and the one son who remained after the death of the father would suffice, with the wife and children he was expected to have, to work the *staxia*, which was doubtless very small in extent, as peasant holdings have usually been in Morea.

186

How a Serf Who Has Remained on Another's Land and Wishes to Leave Can Take Along His Personal Effects.

When a serf acquires some object on another person's land while living there, and his lord wishes to take him back from that place, he can take with him the goods which he had originally brought and those he has acquired, provided he has acknowledged his lord and continues to do so. But if he has not acknowledged him, the lord of the said land can keep the goods. And if the true lord of the serf has commended these goods along with the person of the man to the lord of the land, in this case the serf shall take these goods with him by reason of the commendation made. And when a serf denies that he is the serf of his lord, the penalty is at the discretion of his lord. And likewise, when a serf is wronged no matter how much by his lord, he cannot lodge a complaint against him with the superior lord nor appeal to him regarding the injury which his lord inflicted.

187

How the Lord Can Put His Own Serf in Prison.

If the lord is so pleased, he can put his own serf in prison or hold him in his house for a night and no more, but, as soon as he is able to, he is required to send him to the prison of the superior lord.

Unless the lord has ordered him not to sell anything, the serf can sell his animals and other movable goods without consulting his lord, provided that he retains a pair of oxen and an ass for the service of his lord and for his sustenance.

188

Concerning the Subjection of a Serf Born in the Country.

If the serf of a lord of the Principality who was born in the country makes himself the subject of someone and is possessed by him for a year and a day, he cannot then place himself under another lord. But his own lord can rightly recall and retain him.

189

CONCERNING THE MARRIAGE OF A MALE AND FEMALE SERF.

If a male and female serf legally contract a marriage, even though the marriage has not been solemnized, their children are not regarded as any the less legitimate.

190

HOW, IF A *STAXIA* IS DIVIDED BETWEEN THE FATHER AND THE SONS, THE LORD INHERITS.

If a *staxia* is divided between the father and a son or sons, or between brothers, one does not succeed the other in its inheritance, but rather their lord inherits. And if it is not divided, the inheritance takes place. And when a division is made between the father and the sons, or between the brothers, in this case each of them is bound to furnish to his lord the complete service, that is, the *dispoticaria*, and the rental which is called the *acrostico* all pay in common for the entire *staxia*, just as before the division.[1]

191

HOW A COPY OF THE TESTIMONIES CANNOT BE REFUSED TO THOSE WHO ARE PARTIES TO A LAWSUIT.

When certain persons litigate among themselves, if they desire a copy of the testimonies produced in the trial, the copy cannot be denied them. And if one brings forward certain witnesses to prove his claim, if he relies upon the production of these witnesses, he shall not be able to present others; but if he is not satisfied with this production, he shall be able to present others.

192

HOW HE WHO FAILS TO PAY HIS *CENS* LATER PAYS IT DOUBLE.

He who fails to pay the *cens* to the Prince one year or two years,

[1] See the note to art. 183.

or three or more, is obliged to pay it double, and other punishment he shall not have.[1]

193

WHO HAS THE RIGHT TO EXAMINE TESTIMONIES.

When one has a suit against a liegeman in a feudal matter and wishes to produce witnesses against him, the lord cannot entrust the examination of the witnesses to other than a liegeman. But if the suit is brought against a man of simple homage, the examination of the witnesses shall be entrusted to one of his peers or to one of his superiors. And if the suit is not feudal but is civil or bourgeois or relates to movable goods, the examination of the witnesses shall be entrusted to whom he wills, provided that he [the examiner] is a freeman.

194

CONCERNING A WOMAN, SERVILE OR FREE, WHO ENTERS INTO MATRIMONY.

This is to be observed, that if a woman, whether servile or free, contracts marriage with a serf or with a Greek landowner, after her husband's death she shall have no dower, because her land is divided among her sons, or among the daughters if she has no sons. And after the division among her sons shall have been made, if one of them shall die without legitimate heirs of his body, the lord of whom he holds the land shall inherit.

195

HOW LIEGEMEN ARE TO BE CITED AND HOW THEY ARE NOT TO BE TORTURED MORE THAN THREE TIMES.

When a liegeman is cited to appear before his lord to answer for his inheritance, he who is to cite him must have at least two liegemen, if he is able to have them, so that they can bear witness

[1] The *cens* was usually the rent paid by the free peasant as a token of the lord's superior right in the land. A double payment was thus hardly a crippling fine.

to the citation. And when a liegeman is to be tortured for some crime, he is not to be tortured more than three times and in the presence of at least three liegemen.

196

He Who Wishes Can Make an Appeal Within Ten Days.

He who wishes can appeal from an injustice or a sentence as soon as he can, within ten days and speaking for himself, and he can follow up his appeal within forty days if he to whom he has appealed is in the Principality. But if the latter is outside he shall have a period of a year. Further, the appeal shall not occur if he to whom it is made is outside of the Principality, unless it is the Prince or someone like the Emperor of Constantinople or King.

197

How the Lord Can Take All of the Movable Goods of His Serf.

In accordance with the custom of the above-mentioned Principality the lord can take all of the movable goods of his male or female serf, if he wishes, and can take further his or her *staxia* and give it to another of his serfs. But he must leave to the deprived serf his sustenance, so that the fief to which the serf belongs is not diminished.

198

A Greek serf cannot be a witness against a liegeman in a criminal case involving life or limb.

199

If by the court of the Prince or of another liegeman it has been judged that a vassal is obliged to prove how he holds his land of his lord, or another like holding, and if a period is not fixed, the passage of time does not bear him prejudice. However, when it pleases him he can establish his proof, unless a period of time has been assigned to him by the court.

200

It is a general rule according to the Usage of the Empire of Romania that in civil, criminal, or feudal cases the loser is not sentenced to pay costs, to the profit of the winner.

201

If a period of time is assigned to a married man in a feudal case which concerns him or his wife and he dies in the meantime, the said period does not in any way prejudice his wife. On the contrary, it is necessary to begin the case anew.

202

The seals recognized by the liegemen of the Prince constitute evidence in justice. And if the question arises whether the said seals are known or not, it belongs to the liegemen to settle it.

203

In accordance with the Custom of the Empire of Romania whoever has a serf or serfs who have run away can seize them in whatever place he finds them in the Principality of Achaia, if he finds them in the land of the Prince or of his barons after having made a request to the Prince or barons who have jurisdiction in that place, provided that these serfs confess to belong to him who asks for them.

204

If property of movable or immovable kind is sold to somebody and he who buys gives a small *tournois* [1] as earnest-money to the seller, if either the seller or the buyer afterward repents and does not wish to bind himself to the transaction, he must pay as penalty for the deposit twenty-five hyperpers.

[1] The *sou tournois* or penny of Tours was a common and standard small coin. It was taken over into the Moreot currency and was minted in Greece at the castle at Glarentza, which was called therefrom Castel Tornese.

205

If a vassal holding feudal land of various lords has placed serfs of one fief upon the land of another fief, where the said serfs have planted vines, and he later dies leaving no heirs, the serfs who planted these vines shall possess them after the death of the vassal, notwithstanding that the fiefs in question have passed to different lords. In truth, the aforementioned serfs shall pay the lord of the land for the vines according to what the planted land requires; and they shall leave the remainder of the *staxia* which they held during the life of the first lord, if their present lord so wishes, or else they shall perform the service for the entire *staxia*.

206

A vassal can put his serf in the prison of the lord of the place, provided that when forty days have passed the vassal shall, as he is bound, provide his serf with bread and water every day. And if the lord of the vassal has a prison, the serf must not be put in another prison, if he does not have the wherewithal to live.

207

The Prince or the baron having jurisdiction can, on the petition of somebody, have the adverse party cited. But he cannot fix the period for the complaining party to prove his claim, in civil, feudal, or criminal cases, without the counsel of the liege lords of his court and the consent of the major part of those who make their residence in the Court.

208

When an object is sold at auction or at a public sale and it is later found that it has been stolen, the former owner can recover it after he has first paid him who bought it in the places above indicated. However, if the thief has been apprehended, in this case he who has bought [the object] has recourse against the thief. And if the thief has nothing with which to pay, the price shall be at the determination of the buyer. And if the object has been sold in a place other than the places specified and later is recognized as having been stolen, it returns to its original owner and the buyer does not recover any of the payment which he has made.

209

If a fief falls to a liege vassal, either a man or a woman, and he or she appears before the lord and asks for the investiture or seizin of that fief at the proper time in observance of the legal period of the Principality, and if the lord is negligent in providing the fief, which in right freely reverts to him [the liege vassal], after a year and a day have passed the vassal lodges his complaint of the wrong done to him before the superior of his lord. If the charge is proved, the homage passes to this superior lord, with the judgment of his court. Furthermore, if the said liegewoman who has been thus wronged contracts marriage before she has lodged her complaint before the superior of her lord, after the solemnization of the marriage her husband shall again request the fief from the lord of his wife, just as if no request had been made by his wife. But if the wife has lodged her complaint before the marriage is solemnized, in this case proceedings shall take place before the superior of the lord of the vassal after the marriage has been solemnized, and the said lord of the vassal shall not longer be invoked.

210

He who does liege or simple homage for the land he holds to somebody to whom this homage does not belong immediately loses the land for which he does the homage, in the judgment of the Court. And if in the Principality the person to whom the homage should be paid, or his vicar, fails to appear, and the land in question is governed by the superior lord, in this case the vassal can do homage to this superior lord, provided that the latter requests him and does not want to give him the seizin of the land if homage is not done to himself. However, the vassal must protest that he is saving the faith and the right of him to whom the homage properly belongs.

211

When a vassal appears before his lord for a fief that falls to him and receives the investiture of this fief but fails to obtain the seizin of this fief within a year and a day and proves negligent in acquiring possession thereof, he loses the fief, and the nearest relative who appears within a year and a day from the time of the inheritance and obtains the possession thereof succeeds to it. However, if a person claims a serf as his man and the latter denies it and if the claimant wins the judgment against the recalcitrant serf, if, nevertheless, through his own fault, he neglects to obtain the seizin of the serf during a year and a day, notwithstanding the previous judgment, he loses the seizin of the serf. Subsequently he can, if he wishes, enter a claim of ownership against the above-mentioned serf.

212

According to the Usage of the Empire of Romania, when a liegeman or liegewoman is to succeed to a fief and presents himself within the prescribed time to his lord in order to be invested, if he has requested his lord once, twice, and three times within the year and a day and the latter refuses to invest him and award the seizin of the land as he is obliged, the vassal shall be able to complain of the injury done him to the superior lord of his lord, after the year and day have passed. And if he proves the charge, the homage passes to the nearest superior lord and this lord must invest the aforesaid vassal, whether a liegeman or liegewoman, and give him the seizin if it is demanded of him.

213

The Prince or any other superior can, without asking his liegemen, order his vassals to do or not to do a certain thing, under pain of being in default to their lord or under penalty of [loss of the] fief. And if the vassal does not obey the commands of his superior, he can impose no other penalty except the seizure of his land; and if the said vassal performs the service for him, the lord is obliged to restore the confiscated land to him who has offered the service to him.

214

If a vassal has sown seed in another's land and has not paid the *zemuro* to the lord of the land but has carried all of the grain into his house, if the lord of the land takes the *zemuro* from his house by force, he loses the *zemuro* and pays double to the superior lord of the place where the violence was done. But if the grain is found in a place of the lord of the land, that is, there where it was sown, he who has the land can take the *zemuro* by his own authority. And if [a serf] lives on the land of the lord of the fief, even as a *nicario*, the lord of the land shall take the *zemuro* in the house of the serf by his own authority.[1]

215

When a serf is in debt to another person for a certain amount of money, by reason of trade or of a loan, if he is unable to pay, his *staxia* must not be sold. But if his lord agrees that the serf engage in trade, that which he has acquired can be sold, even the immovable goods, except the *staxia*, in order to satisfy the creditor. And if he lacks the wherewithal to pay, he shall be put in prison on the petition of his creditor. However, if the lord of the serf orders him not to engage in trade, or that no one should lend him money, and if, after the order that has been given him, the serf engages in commerce or contracts a loan and does not have the wherewithal to pay, he cannot be put in prison on the petition of his creditor, nor can he who has made him a loan demand anything. But if the serf is not a tradesman and is somebody's debtor, he is obliged to pay his debts; and for this, his movable goods shall be sold, a pair of oxen and an ass being kept for him. But he cannot be put in prison if the debt was not made with the permission of his lord.

216

When a baron, or some other lord, who has liegemen under him, with malevolent intention and through his own fault lays a hand on his liegeman so as to injure him, the liegeman can rightly, if he

[1] For *zemuro* see the note to art. 37; *nicario*, art. 181.

wishes, make his complaint before the superior lord of his lord against the injury which he has suffered. And if he proves it, after the judgment his ligeance passes to the immediate superior of his lord.

217

If a female vassal has a daughter and this daughter has a son or daughter by some man while her mother is living, and it happens that the daughter of the female vassal dies before her mother, while her son and daughter are still minors, and before she has been invested with her mother's fief, her husband shall not have the guardianship of the land, which belongs to his children. But that one shall be the guardian who is to succeed to the land if the children should die without heirs. And the same thing shall occur if the aforementioned vassal predeceases her daughter and her daughter dies before she has been invested with her mother's fief, because the husband shall not have the guardianship of the land belonging to the children of himself and his wife, but that one shall be the guardian who is to succeed to the fief.

218

In How Many Ways the Term "Guardian" Is Used.

The term "guardian" is used in many ways: namely, of the lord of a vassal when he has wardship; of the relative nearest in degree; of the mother or father; of the husband who has the guardianship of his wife, to whom feudal land belongs either by inheritance or as dower.

219

What Should Be Done When a Serf Commits a Crime and Does Not Want to Answer a Summons?

When a serf commits a crime for which he is liable to a penalty of mutilation or of loss of life and when summoned refuses to appear, his property must not, by reason of this crime or his contempt of court, be seized or confiscated, because to all of his movable and immovable goods the lord of the serf succeeds, just as to the goods of his slave.[1] And the same is even to be observed if the serf commits treason or another crime, namely, that his goods pass to his lord, even though the serf is not to suffer capital punishment, that is, decapitation.

EXPLICIT LIBER
DE CONSUETUDINIBUS IMPERII ROMANIE.
DEO GRATIAS.

[1] We say, perhaps arbitrarily, "slave" for *servo* in the original. *Servo* in this context does not necessarily mean that there were slaves in thirteenth or fourteenth century Morea; the clause is added possibly as a hypothetical example to emphasize the point that the lord alone succeeds to his serf's goods. In this article, as throughout the code, we consistently say "serf" where the original has *villano*. Recoura translates *vilain* throughout (and *serf* for *servo* in art. 219), but we strongly doubt that he could have demonstrated that the Moreot peasant enjoyed the status of the contemporary French *vilain*. The unmistakably servile traits of the Moreot peasant (which we summarize in the Commentary under "Justice") justify our rendition of *villano* as "serf." The Moreot peasant who pays a *cens* (cf. art. 192), rather than the *villano*, may better be equated with the French *vilain*. Needless to add, it is notoriously difficult to distinguish clearly, in terms of legal and economic status, between the various groups and classes of medieval peasants in any country or period.

COMMENTARY ON FEUDAL INSTITUTIONS IN FRANKISH GREECE AND IN MEDIEVAL EUROPE AS REVEALED IN THE ASSIZES OF ROMANIA

COMMENTARY

THE following sketch is a commentary on the main features of medieval feudalism as suggested in the Assizes of Romania. "Feudalism" is one of the larger terms of the historian's vocabulary whose careless application makes difficult the understanding of the history and institutions of medieval Europe. The word loses a good deal of its meaning if used as a label for the whole period between Charlemagne and the fourteenth or fifteenth century—a period of rapid change and of great variety of ideas and institutions. Unfortunately it is difficult to give any precise definition, partly because our scanty sources do not give us a clear picture of feudal origins, and partly because feudal institutions themselves varied widely from country to country and changed rapidly within most of these countries. A corollary difficulty is the interpretation of the significance of feudal institutions—as for example, their importance in the constitutional development of the emerging national states of the later medieval period. In spite of these difficulties, there is a wide area of agreement among historians concerning the essential and characteristic elements of feudalism. Most fundamental was vassalage, the close and highly honorable relationship between two men implying mutual faith and loyalty. A long evolution lay back of vassalage. One influence was the Roman practice whereby clients sought to improve their economic and social position by commending themselves to rich and influential patrons. A more decisive influence was the ancient Germanic institution of the *comitatus*, an association of free warriors led by a chieftain to whom they gave such complete loyalty that it was disgraceful to survive him unavenged if he were struck down in battle. A second basic element of feudalism was the fief, the landed estate which a vassal held of a lord as payment for stipulated services. Its immediate ancestor was the "benefice" and more remotely the *precaria* of the Merovingian Franks and imperial Romans, which was a grant of land in return for rent or service; since it might be ended at any time the tenure was "precarious" or conditional. The genesis of feudalism lies in the special association of vassalage with benefice-holding on a wide scale which becomes characteristic of the Carolingian kingdom in the eighth century and was due to a third fundamental element of feudalism, that of specialized military service by heavily armed horsemen. When the military exigencies of the empire, especially the warfare with the Saracens, forced Charles Martel to raise large forces of heavily armed cavalry, he did so by creating many new benefices out of confiscated church lands and granting them to vassals, who thus had the means of arming and equipping themselves. Since fighting on horseback was very expensive and since such vassals could only be paid in the form of large estates (at a time when the economy of western Europe was almost purely agricultural), it is easy to see that the feudal vassals formed an exalted warlike aristocracy socially far above the mass of peasants and serfs. This status carried with it corresponding political and judicial privileges which the greater vassals consolidated during the period of the disintegration of the centralized authority of the Carolingian kings. These privileges (called collectively the "immunity") may be regarded as still another basic element of feudalism. The great fief was in effect a unit of local or regional government; the later Carolingian monarchs proved unable to undo or limit the usurpation and exercise of governmental powers by fief-holders, who thus made a private possession of public authority.

These several institutions and practices which we can properly call feudal resulted in a new organization of society. A class of warriors dominated the politics and social life of Europe for several centuries and went far in "feudalizing" the Christian Church, the single most important medieval institution. The political, military, and legal relationships of the members of this class, which constitute the actual feudal institutions, have been recorded in a fairly large number of compilations of customs and laws. One of these "custumals" is the Assizes of Romania, the text of which, presented in English translation above, is the occasion of the present commentary.

HOMAGE AND FEALTY

The Assizes begin appropriately with a discussion of homage and fealty, the two elements of the ceremony that established the all-important bond between lord and vassal. In this bond we see the peculiarity of feudalism as a system of government—the quality which makes it appear strange to the modern subject of an impersonal and sovereign state. For through the act of homage and fealty two men entered into an intimate social and political union out of which flowed important practical consequences. The successful administration of the large Carolingian kingdom depended on the loyalty of a relatively small number of great vassals to the monarch. William the Conqueror ruled England firmly because of the unquestioned fidelity of the group of barons to whom he had distributed fiefs scattered through a large conquered country. One of the old French feudal epics, Raoul de Cambrai, affords a very striking example of the strength of the bond of vassalage. Raoul has invaded lands belonging to the family of his squire, Bernier, ignoring the latter's protests, and goes to the extreme of burning a monastery and causing the death of Bernier's mother, a nun. Bernier and his father avenge her death, Bernier himself slaying Raoul. Yet Bernier can take no satisfaction in the act—he has killed his own lord, who had knighted him and to whom he feels more closely bound than to his own parents. Many years later the remorseful squire is appropriately killed by Raoul's nephew close to the scene of Raoul's death.

Like many medieval ceremonies, homage and fealty was a solemn and highly formal transaction. It was much the same throughout feudal Europe and the Latin Orient. The description of the homage ritual in the Assizes of Romania (arts. 3 and 68) is brief but complete, except for the vassal's act of kneeling and placing his clasped hands in those of the lord at the beginning. This symbolical act of submission, together with the vassal's declaring himself the man of his lord for a designated fief, is the decisive element in the ceremony—it constituted the solemn "engagement of vassalage." After the lord had raised the vassal to his feet and had kissed him on the mouth, it was usual for the vassal to swear fealty, on the Gospels or other sacred object, by way of confirming the declaration of homage proper. Fealty was so completely implied in homage that some of the custumals omit specific mention of it. Frequently homage and fealty were confounded or considered synonymous, as in article 65 of the Assizes. The kiss bestowed on the vassal indicates that lord and vassal remain social equals, regardless of any submission or subordination that was implied in doing homage.

An act so solemn and binding as homage must be done in person by the two principals. One cannot be too careful in doing homage—it must be done to the right person, for the right fief, and in the strictly prescribed manner. Article 210 admits of an exception but strongly emphasizes that the vassal must "save" his loyalty for the correct lord. Quite understandably, a woman could not do homage in person, since the act implied the obligation to serve the lord in war and risk life itself; here a substitute, usually the woman's husband, was provided. Article 61 suggests a reason peculiar to the crusading East for enforcing the performance of homage in person: if custom had allowed the heirs of crusader fiefs to do homage by proxy, many of them would have remained in the West as absentee lords, depriving their states of badly needed defenders. A chapter in John d'Ibelin's treatise (172 *bis*) offers a close parallel to article 61. The requirement that the Prince of Morea must personally receive the homage and fealty of his vassals and subjects (art. 2) received special emphasis after the principality was ceded to the Angevins (1267–78). The Moreot lieges would not do homage to the bailiff of a distant ruler, neither of whom could know the customs of the land well and rule in its true interest. Hence the dramatic scene, described in the Greek Chronicle of Morea, in which the assembled prelates, barons, and knights of Morea, through their spokesman, Archbishop Benedict of Patras, rebuffed the first Angevin bailiff (1278) when he demanded their homage. The question was evaded by a compromise whereby the bailiff swore on the Gospels to rule by the customs of the land, and the Moreots swore to be faithful and true to Anjou and his bailiff—but did not perform homage as such (art. 136). We hear of actual homage being done only when resident princes appointed by the king of Naples, like Florent d'Avesnes and Philip of Savoy, ruled the principality. The oath which the prince or bailiff (arts. 1, 136) took before his vassals to maintain the "franchises and usages" of Morea has reference to the principality as an Angevin dependency. The Chronicle of Morea records very similar oaths taken of Florent and Philip when they assumed their rule. The Achaian barons were probably just as vigilant for their privileges under the male Villehardouin princes as they were during the Angevin period. Indeed, this vigilance for their customs and for their specific grants and privileges strongly characterizes the public law of all of the crusading foundations. John d'Ibelin records that the king of Jerusalem swore before his men to uphold not only the usages and assizes generally but also the grants and privileges made by his predecessors (chap. 193). No clause similar to the last occurs in the oaths of the kings of France, England, and Germany. But in the Orient too little time had elapsed—four or five generations when Ibelin wrote—since the original infeudations, and the vassals were anxious that each sovereign confirm them by solemn oath.

"The other subjects must take an oath of fealty" (art. 2). The tie of fealty between ruler and subject antedated the development of feudalism in the West and persisted in the feudal period, when it strengthened the bond between lord and vassal established through homage, and constituted a general nexus between the suzerain and the non-noble inhabitants of his realm. Eventually, in the monarchies of France and England, as feudal ties became weak or ineffective, all subjects were bound to the king by a bond of loyalty as expressed in an oath of "allegiance"—a word which derives from "ligeance" in the sense of an unconditioned loyalty to the feudal lord. But such a "modern" state of things is very far from the feudalism of thirteenth-century Achaia. Nevertheless the germ of it is visible in the oath that his non-noble subjects swore to the prince, as well as in the fealty sworn by his vassals: that is another way of pointing out the distinctively feudal character of homage.

Originally a vassal did exclusive, unconditioned homage to one lord, his only lord, whom he personally served in battle and whose court he attended. But at an early time, through grants from other lords, inheritance or other means, vassals acquired more than one fief, and this brought about various modifications of the original homage. In most feudal states a distinction between *liege,* and *simple* or *ordinary* homage was established. A vassal with many fiefs did liege homage to one lord, whom he would alone serve in person, while performing homage to the other lords on the basis of various conditions, like providing substitutes for service in the lord's army and court, and being excused from one or another of the main feudal obligations. As the Assizes of Romania make clear, homage to the liege lord must always be saved. However, feudal relationships became so complicated that a vassal might have several liege lords. In such a case a vassal in practice had paramount obligations to a particular liege lord, on the basis, for example, of the fief longest in the possession of his family, or the fief where he made his chief residence, or some other distinction (cf. art. 99). Actually, by the thirteenth century in most feudal states, liege homage had become the regular type of homage, and a vassal might do any number of ligeances, always reserving the previous ones.

Certainly in Morea liege homage was the only type of homage which was properly feudal. The Assizes of Romania speak frequently of "liege" and "simple" or "plain" homage, but it is clear from articles 72, 68, and others that the simple homager was a distinctly inferior feudatory. He did homage through an oath instead of the ritual of symbolic subjection of liege homage. Nor could he subinfeudate, hold a court, or even attend the court of his lord. Possibly some of the Greek feudatories had the status of simple homagers. Or they may all have been Westerners who were simple knights with very small holdings who provided military service (art. 71) but otherwise lacked most of the traits and powers of a feudal seignior.

INVESTITURE AND SEIZIN: DISSEIZIN

At the same time that the vassal does homage he is invested with the fief by the lord (cf. art. 68). The two acts may be regarded as the indispensable parts of a single process; together they create the feudal relationship. Investiture with a rod, hood, glove, or other object was the symbolic transference of the fief from lord to vassal. In the earliest period of feudalism grantor and grantee went to the land itself and the vassal pointed it out as the fief he was henceforth to hold. In Morea as in the feudal world generally from the twelfth century on, this ceremony was replaced by a written document recording the grant.[1] Investiture must ordinarily be sought within forty days and at the longest within a year (arts. 61, 120, 121). The Greek feudatories, apparently (art. 138), were not bound by these limits; perhaps some Roman-Byzantine method of proving possession prevailed among them.

Investiture as such, however, does not make possession certain. As the Assizes repeatedly state, "seizin" of the land in question for a year and a day is necessary. That is, there must be physical possession of the land and the cultivation and enjoyment of it for this period (cf. especially art. 211). One of the earliest assizes of the Kingdom of Jerusalem, that is, a formal statement of existing custom, which goes back to the reign of Godfrey de Bouillon (1099–1100), declares that after possession of a year and a day the fief-holder could not be disturbed in his enjoyment of the land. Annual possession was the old Germanic prescription which brought virtual ownership and persisted in many of the feudal customaries. Article 9 of the Assizes prohibits the prince or any official of his from disseizing the tenant who has had possession for a year and day.

If disseizin has taken place unjustly, the following procedure is open to the victim: He must request his fief from the disseizing lord three times in one year, demanding judgment of his peers in the lord's court, and if at the end of the year his fief has not been restored to him in full seizin his homage automatically passes to the nearest superior lord. However, if the disseized is a man of simple homage he can bring suit for recovery in the court of his

[1] When, at the end of the Akova case (see note to art. 36), William de Villehardouin regranted a third of the barony to Marguerite de Passavant, he ordered that a "Frankish privilege" be drawn up, that is, a charter describing the grant, sealed by the chancellor. William placed it under the quilt of his bed and had Marguerite summoned to his presence. He then withdrew the charter, handed it to her, and invested her with his glove. (The glove stood for the prince's control of the land—his power to grant.) A second charter was then drawn up granting the remaining two-thirds of the barony of Akova to William's daughter. (The rather quaint description of these proceedings is to be found in the Greek Chronicle of Morea [Schmitt ed.], ll. 7673–7752.)

superior lord once forty days have passed. But the liege must be long suffering; if he brings suit before a year has passed he loses his fief. He is like the vassal of the *Laws of Henry I* (of England), who must bear the injustice of his lord for thirty days in war, for a year and day in peace.

The decision of the court of the immediate or superior lord in Morea virtually settles the question of ownership as well as that of possession. The simpler feudal custom of Morea and Jerusalem did not develop any possessory actions for the recovery of land as did the Anglo-Norman law in the twelfth century and French law in the thirteenth. These actions are due to the initiative and strength of central authority, that of duke or king, acting in the interest of greater public order and security of property. The best-known among them are the so-called assizes of *novel disseisin* and *mort d'ancestor*, which were writs drawn up in the chancery of Henry II of England enabling their purchasers to decide questions of disputed possession before royal justices. In the case of the writ of *novel disseisin* (that is, recent dispossession), the sheriff was directed to summon "twelve free and lawful men of the neighborhood" and to put them on oath to answer the question whether the claimant was disseized as of a recent date. If the answer were affirmative he was immediately repossessed. The fact of recent possession alone was settled, and frequently the dispute went no further. If the defeated party felt he had been wronged he could resort to a so-called Writ of Right which initiated a more complicated action to investigate the dispute more thoroughly and decide who had a better right to the land. Jerusalem developed an action comparable to *novel disseisin* but only for subvassals seeking recourse in the baronial court; and even here, arbitration out of court was the usual solution. An action of *novel disseisin* had to be brought within forty days after the dispossession. We may compare with this the requirement that the simple homager of Morea seek restitution within forty days and start action in the court of the higher lord immediately thereafter (art. 49). Article 9 of the Assizes asks in closing if the dispossessed heir who has held a year and day is entitled to judgment. The answer is that the annual prescription protects him, but one wonders what recourse the Moreot heir would have had who had been in possession less than a year and day—or had been prevented entirely from coming into possession. In England after 1176 he had the assize of *mort d'ancestor,* which enabled him to act at once before the royal justices, frequently against his ancestor's lord, who had prevented his succession. By this action twelve neighbors were empaneled as a jury to answer if the claimant's ancestor had possessed the disputed land on the day he died and if the claimant were the nearest heir. These and other possessory assizes became justly popular in England. Not only did they provide better justice than the baronial courts, but they also helped to make trial by jury a normal part of the procedure in the royal courts. Obviously the modern trial jury has not evolved unchanged from its ancestor; the efficacy of the latter lay in the special knowledge which the neighbors had, while in the modern jury a premium is placed on the jurors' ignorance of the facts of the case.

THE FIEF

Although vassalage was the most essential element of feudalism, without which European feudalism could not have come into being, the most common institution of the new society was the fief. It is from the Latin form of the word (*feodum, feudum*) that the very terms "feudal" and "feudalism" derive. The fief in its various aspects is a summary of the peculiar features of feudalism. In its earliest use the word designated the military benefice, the Latin term for which (*beneficium*) it eventually replaced. For one thing the benefice or fief was an agrarian estate granted by the Carolingian ruler to a military retainer, the vassal, to be held by the latter on condition of providing service as a heavy-armed horseman. While the vassal made free use of the land, it was not his to dispose of. The Roman notion of the absolute ownership of property was foreign to the old Germanic conception, which admitted only of the possession of land. Possession if proved against one claimant was no guarantee against the claim of a third or fourth person. This conception received peculiar emphasis in the fief. The earliest fiefs were granted so conditionally that they might be revoked while grantor and grantee were still living. Even after the fief became hereditary it was always necessary for the successor to be invested with his ancestor's fief. Grants made only for a number of years or for the lifetime of either the grantor or the grantee continued to be made throughout the feudal period. Such are the grants described in articles 98 and 134 of the Assizes of Romania. Article 112 of the same Assizes speaks of the grant of a fief to a grantee and his heirs—this we may regard as the "normal" or "permanent" type of feudal grant lasting for several generations.

Already we have seen that two persons had rights in the same estate, the Carolingian ruler, that is, the lord (grantor), and the vassal (grantee). But the latter might himself make a grant—that is, subinfeudate—to a third person, and the third to a fourth, whose holding might only suffice to support himself and his family. It was called his *demesne* land, and each lord above him in the scale of dependent tenure retained the ungranted portion of his estate as his demesne, for his personal support. These lands were worked by free peasants paying a rental or by unfree serfs. All of the inhabitants, noble and non-noble, had a stake in the land, a right of possession protected by custom, but none had any rights equivalent to full ownership.

Thus we see that the large estate or fief granted by the ruler to a powerful vassal is subdivided in order to raise a fighting force. Had the Carolingian rulers been liberally supplied with cash they could have hired their troops. But in the almost purely agricultural economy of their time the most convenient form in which to pay their vassals was grants of land. Actually the fief did take other forms, especially with the advent of a money economy in the twelfth and thirteenth centuries, such as grants of customs receipts, of tithes and of rights of coinage, or of a public office with its perquisites. But the fief was much more than a unit of income. Its holder enjoyed various rights of administration, justice, and taxation over its inhabitants. The large fief resembled a regional or local unit of government of a modern state. But the resemblance can be very deceptive. The powerful vassal thought of his "sovereignty" as a private possession which he would try to pass on to his heirs, and parts of which he might allow subordinate vassals to exercise. Even the lowliest vassal had certain governmental rights over his peasants and serfs, especially in the realm of justice. A private agreement between lord and vassal fixed their respective rights. The king of France in the thirteenth century, like his contemporary the prince of Morea, was the most powerful person of the country because he was the largest landholder. Royal or princely powers that we think of in terms of public or constitutional law were an amplification of private rights. The historian who traces the growth of the national administrative system or of parliament in medieval England must take into account the private household of the king and the law of the tenure of fiefs.

The fief, then, was the central institution of feudal society—it determined a man's wealth and office and political power, as well as his social status and place in the feudal hierarchy. Significantly the word "honor" came into wide use as a synonym for fief: a man derived distinction from his fief. The degree of feudalization, that is, the extent to which all available land and political authority was brought under the conception of the fief, varied widely from country to country or area to area. England in this respect may be regarded as the perfectly feudalized country. All the land of England was held by someone of someone else, and directly or indirectly all held of the king. In the northern half of France also feudalization went very far, giving rise to the saying "*nulle terre sans seigneur*" ("no land without its lord"). But even here alodial land—that is, land held in absolute ownership—was to be found. In southern France, as well as in Germany and Italy (including the Norman South and Sicily), alods were much more numerous. In Morea we have to reckon with the imperfectly feudalized holdings of the Greek "archons" or landowners; Jerusalem, however, presents a high degree of feudalization.

MILITARY SERVICE

The fief came into being in order to provide heavy-armed cavalrymen—knights—for the armies of the Carolingian monarchs. During the several centuries that knights had a monopoly of military power, the fief remained a most important unit of economic and social organization. Unfortunately we have little information about the exact nature and organization of military service in relation to the fief—at least until national records become abundant for France and England in the thirteenth century. The normal situation was for lord and vassal to have an oral understanding on the military requirements of the particular fief. The vassal's peers, holding of the same lord, who witnessed the homage and investiture ceremony that bound their lord and fellow vassal, were available to confirm the arrangements. It is certain that in no feudal state did there prevail any standard unit or amount of land by which knight service was measured. There was no fixed proportion between the size and value of land and the amount of service. The duchy of Normandy probably made the closest approach of any feudal state to a system of distribution of fiefs in which the amount of service was proportionate to the value of the feudal land. English feudalism, although it was implanted by the Normans, presents no uniformity in this regard. The English kings expected a stipulated number of knights from each tenant-in-chief but in allocating the number of knights' fees there was no standard conception of what constituted a knight's fee, that is, the holding of a single knight, so that the size of the barony and the number of fees had no necessary relation. The subinfeudations made by the royal vassals presented great variations—a subvassal of social position close to that of the tenant-in-chief or otherwise favored by the latter might owe the service of one knight for a fief many times the value of another grant owing the identical service. Similar variations prevailed in other feudal states, although a tendency toward uniformity no doubt was always present, especially among the vassals of the same large fief, who were one another's peers.

Military service took two chief forms—actual service in the field, and castle-guard. The former might involve service on large expeditions against domestic or foreign enemies, with the entire feudal array of the country serving under the ruler. It might also involve less important expeditions of short duration, as when the vassal fought for his immediate lord against a rival lord. The French words *ost* and *chevauchée* are often used to designate these two occasions of service respectively, but often enough they were both used imprecisely in the sense of a military expedition. Article 26 of the Assizes of Romania seems to distinguish between *ost* and *chevauchée*. The occasion for *chevauchée* in Morea could be petty private warfare between the French lords, or more often, local conflict with the Greeks. *Ost* would usually be the "general expedition" under the Prince against the Greeks of Mistrâ, especially after 1262. We may surmise that a longer period than fifteen days was allowed the vassal to prepare for an expedition outside the principality.

The importance of castle-guard is sometimes under-estimated in considering the subject of military service. The castle, whether the wooden motte-and-bailey type or the later elaborate stone structure, frequently played a decisive role in offensive and especially defensive warfare. Feudal custom carefully regulated the construction and control of castles. The French developed a rather elaborate special custom dealing with the "rendition" or giving up of castles to the suzerain at his request. The actual waiting or watching in the castle might be done by peasants in France, while the noble held to castle-guard served by taking up his residence in the lord's castle for a certain period. In England, where the castle was extremely important as part of the system of national defense in the later eleventh and twelfth centuries, the service of knights in castles is well attested. The "private" castles of the barons lost their importance during the reign of Henry II, whose own castles together with hired troops sufficed for national defense.

In the crusading East, which was in a state of virtually constant warfare with outside enemies, the castle had a crucial importance, and the great stone fortresses of Jerusalem seem to have exercised a definite influence on western architecture. The king had a theoretical control over all castles but often enough proved too weak to exercise it. Both the prince of Morea (Assizes, art. 19) and the king of Jerusalem must consult with their lieges before disposing of a castle. Not only could the king not deliver a castle into Saracen hands but he could neither sell nor give a fortress to the Church or the military-religious orders. His lieges were empowered, without violating their fealty, to prevent him from carrying out such acts. Greece is still covered with ruins of Frankish fortresses built at countless strategic points. Thanks to the highly mountainous character of the country castles were indispensable as a means of keeping the natives in subjection and providing defense against external attack by land or sea. Several references in the Assizes of Romania to castles and castle-guard point up their importance (cf.

arts. 19, 26, 94). The limitation of castle-building to the prince and the twelve barons who have "blood-justice" is emphatically stated in article 94.

The precise conditions of military service varied considerably in the feudal world, perhaps in no respect more than in the duration of service, which was practically unlimited in early feudalism but tended increasingly to be limited. Normandy was the earliest to develop the forty-day limitation in the eleventh century. It was widely imitated in the rest of France and England, and was summed up concisely in the "establishment" of St. Louis (1270):

> The baron and all vassals of the king are bound to appear before him when he shall summon them, and to serve him at their own expense for forty days and forty nights, with as many knights as each one owes; and he is able to exact from them these services when he wishes and when he has need of them. And if the king wishes to keep them more than forty days at their own expense, they are not bound to remain if they do not wish it. And if the king wishes to keep them at his expense for the defense of the realm, they are bound to remain. And if the king wishes to lead them outside of the kingdom, they need not go unless they wish to, for they have already served their forty days and forty nights.

The corresponding limitation in German feudalism was six weeks' service at the vassal's expense, and beyond that at the lord's.

The crusading states never enjoyed sufficient peace to be able to develop limitations of service comparable to those of the West. The annual service required of Moreot liegemen, defined in article 70 of the Assizes, receives confirmation in the Chronicle of Morea, which adds that the holders of four fiefs must provide one knight and twelve squires, and those holding a large number must provide for each extra fief one knight or two mounted squires.[1] A fairly

[1] A charter of 1303 shows Philip of Savoy and his wife Isabelle de Villehardouin, the princess of Achaia, making a grant to their daughter Marguerite of the important castle and castellany of Karytaina and of Bucelet, in Arcadia, in return for "the service of her body and of six knights, six months in the year." Perhaps the shorter period of six months was an exception in Marguerite's favor, in view of her relationship to the grantees; it was still, of course, a long period in itself. (Charter in J. A. Buchon, *Recherches historiques sur la principauté française de Morée et ses hautes baronnies* [2 vols., Paris, 1845], II, 381.)

large number of knights, or "sergeants of the conquest," as the chronicler calls them (whom he says he cannot stop to name individually), each received a grant for which they owed "service with their own body." The Chronicle also explains the division of Morea at the conquest into twelve large fiefs or baronies, the largest of which, Akova, owed the service of twenty-four knights. The archbishop of Patras owed eight knights, and the six bishops four apiece. The Templars, Hospitallers, and Teutonic Knights likewise owed four knights each for their lands.[2] The military-religious orders in Morea do not have anything like the military importance of their counterparts in Jerusalem.

A number of articles of the Assizes give us some interesting details about the nature of military service in Morea—the insistence that mounted service can be exacted only from a knight's fief (29); when personal service is required (53, 126); retirement of the Moreot knight at sixty (if he has survived to this remarkable old age for a feudal warrior!) (89); the equation: one knight = two squires, and the service of one squire for a sergeanty (67), etc. The lord must not give his vassal an impossible military assignment (22), and he must reduce the service if the vassal's fief is diminished in war (65). An assize of King Amaury I of Jerusalem (*Assise de Belfis*) specified that a vassal need not follow his lord in a siege operation where his horse could not carry him—a provision intended probably to prevent the loss of knights as infantry in storming a castle or city walls. Jerusalem made great use of the custom known as *restor*, of which we have no record in the practices of Morea. In its broadest meaning *restor* might be any replacement of equipment lost by a knight while serving his lord. But by the end of the thirteenth century it was limited exclusively

[2] Greek Chronicle, Schmitt ed., ll. 1912–2009; French Chronicle, Longnon ed., pars. 128–29. The Aragonese version of the Chronicle (Morel-Fatio, ed.) describes the fiefs and their services somewhat differently, using as its source the register of fiefs as it existed a long time after the time of the conquest. Unlike William the Conqueror, who carved out fiefs for his followers as he proceeded through England, the Franks, after their rapid conquest of Morea, had the leisure to set up a commission of ten to determine the feudal division of the land. Besides Geoffrey I de Villehardouin this commission consisted of two Latin bishops, two bannerets (who ranked between ordinary knights and the twelve peers of the prince), and five important Greek landowners. (Greek Chronicle, 1830 ff.)

to the practice of restoring mutilated or slain horses at the lord's expense. Freedom from this major economic worry obviously was a large factor in sustaining the morale of the feudal warrior.

The spatial limitation of service was sometimes an even greater concern of the vassal than the temporal. Article 65 of the Assizes opens with a general statement of the point. Both in law and practice the Jerusalemite custom limited service outside the country. But here as in all feudal states the lord could have his way if he bore the vassal's expenses. When the kingdom of Jerusalem included Cyprus the problem of service in the two parts of a realm separated by the sea became an acutely disputed question, as in the case of the Anglo-Norman barons with holdings on both sides of the Channel. In England the controversy takes its place among the irritations that helped to cause the break between John and the barons of Magna Carta. The question was never directly settled in England, but the commutation of service into a money payment was an indirect solution.

Commutation of military service (known as "scutage" in England) became a very widespread practice by the end of the thirteenth century. By enabling rulers to hire troops and officials it became a major factor in the decline of feudalism, whose ruling class had for centuries dominated the army and administration. The earliest reference to scutage is in 1100, and during the course of the twelfth century it was frequently resorted to both by the king vis-à-vis his direct vassals, and by the latter vis-à-vis their own tenants. Both in England and France the important lords encouraged commutation. It is misleading to think that the kings alone encouraged the custom in the interests of weakening the baronage. Among other reasons, the practical difficulties involved in "bringing out" a feudal army—in seeing that every one owing service had answered his lord's summons and was fully equipped at the right time and place—made commutation appeal to any ruler or baron who had the responsibility of summoning a large number of knights. *Pari passu* with commutation went the increased granting of money-fiefs as commerce revived, by which rulers could bind a large number of new "liegemen" to themselves on more desirable terms of military service than the holders of landed fiefs were obliged to observe. The commercial prosperity of the crusading states, even though most of it redounded to the benefit of the Italian cities, enabled their rulers to bestow a large number of money-fiefs on vassals. The remarkable seigniory which Count Joscelyn III de Courtenay built up in Jerusalem in the 1170's and 1180's was in part the result of several grants of money-fiefs against the revenues of port towns. We know of money-fiefs granted by the prince of Morea against the revenues of the port of Glarentza, which in the fourteenth century was an important Mediterranean port, with its own recognized weights and measures and the official mint of the principality. The military forces of both Morea and Jerusalem became highly mercenary and correspondingly non-feudal, including bodies of troops raised from native peoples of the Near East and paid for periods of indefinite service.

THE FEUDAL HIERARCHY AND THE GRAND OFFICERS

In France there is no well-defined hierarchy among the higher feudatories until the twelfth and thirteenth centuries. The rulers of the most powerful states are variously titled duke, count, viscount, or simply lord. Thus a tenth-century count of Barcelona inconsistently styled himself count, duke, marquis, and prince. Rank was determined by effective power, whose main elements were extensive landed possessions, the prestige of the ruler, and a dependable array of vassals. The *count* of Flanders was a greater lord than the *duke* of Burgundy. In 1066 the duke of Normandy was a far more powerful feudatory than the nominal king of France. The proud boast—concealed beneath mock humility—of the ruler of the seigniory of Couci was: "I am neither count nor marquis, I am the lord of Couci!"

It took the patient effort of several able rulers to turn the nominal authority of the supreme feudatory—the Capetian king—into an effective suzerainty. At the same time the titles borne by the important feudatories tended to correspond more accurately to the relative importance of their states. The feudal pyramid of lords and vassals became a truly graduated hierarchy under Philip Augustus, who mastered even the duchy of Normandy. When in 1185 he took possession of the county of Amiens, which was the fief of the church of Amiens, he purchased from the church the right to be quit of doing homage to it: the crown must not be vassal of anybody. In Germany it became a rule that a feudatory could not hold a fief of one who was of inferior rank.

By the thirteenth century the hierarchy had been systematized in France. A lawbook of St. Louis' time lists the following ranks beneath the king: duke, marquis, count, viscount, baron, castellan, and vavassor.[1] The title "baron" here has a restricted meaning, to designate the lord who is not entitled to the dignity of viscount. But for a long time in most of the feudal world it designated any important vassal, especially one holding directly of the king or of the territorial prince or ruler. Such was the usage in Morea, where the first rank in the hierarchy beneath the prince was occupied by the eleven "barons of the land," as the Chronicle calls those who, along with the prince, held the twelve large fiefs into which the peninsula was divided at the conquest. A class of lesser feudatories stood in liege relationship to the prince and to the barons. The lowest rung of the feudal ladder was occupied by the numerous class of men of simple homage—the ordinary knights, who were rather sharply distinguished from the liegemen and barons.[2]

Greek landlords ("archons") comprised a special group in the feudal aristocracy of Morea (cf. Assizes, arts. 71, 138, 178, 194). Their mention in the Assizes of Romania confirms the statements of the Chronicle of Morea that those native landlords who came to terms with the Frankish conquerors retained their lands and privileges. Grants made to them were permanent, and what is rather remarkable, their lands were subject to equal inheritance rather

[1] The vavassor in thirteenth-century France is generally a simple knight holding a small fief with, at most, powers of low justice over his tenants, but having no vassals of his own.

[2] The title of "prince" was rather rare among feudal rulers. The word was used in the plural in France to refer to the important lords of a feudal state, somewhat like the use of "baron." In Germany the title was restricted in the twelfth century to the magnates who held directly of the king. Innocent III referred to Geoffrey I de Villehardouin as prince in his letters, and Geoffrey used the title in his private acts. It was probably no more than the accident of the usage of the papal chancery that led to the adoption of the title. It certainly did not possess at the beginning the implications of sovereignty and independence which attached to the title of "prince of Antioch" as used by Bohemund I and his successors. (Cf. Jean Longnon, "Problèmes de l'histoire de la principauté de Morée," *Journal des Savants*, April–June, 1946, pp. 83–84.)

than primogeniture, even in the case of a Frankish vassal married to a Greek lady. Like the Franks, the Greek nobles were subject to military service. They fought with William de Villehardouin at Pelagonia in 1259. We are told by the Aragonese version of the Chronicle of Morea that Geoffrey de Bruyères, the lord of Karytaina, while engaged in border warfare with the imperial Greek forces of Mistrâ in 1264, was ably assisted by Greek noblemen whom he had "nourished and fostered" and who had done homage to him. They conspicuously proved their loyalty on this occasion and were rewarded with new grants of land, while the noblest among them were knighted by Geoffrey.[3]

The highest feudatories of Morea are also referred to as peers of the prince in article 43 of the Assizes, along with the seigniors of certain states in Continental Greece and the islands, who acknowledged the suzerainty of the prince. These Moreot peers are among the eleven great barons of Morea enfeoffed at the conquest and enjoying rights of high justice, as we learn from article 94. Together with the Villehardouins they constituted twelve peers, in imitation of the apostolic number and of the "douze pers" of Charlemagne and the French epic. Inasmuch as the Moreot peers dominated the High Court and were one another's judges, we can trace no special development in Achaia to parallel that of the twelve peers of the French kings in the thirteenth century. In the face of the rapidly growing royal authority the French peers tried to prevent the grand officers of the crown from being judges with them in cases involving the peers. The crown, however, won its point, the peers failing to secure any substantial political and judicial prerogatives.[4]

[3] *Libro de los fechos et conquistas del principado de la Morea* . . . (ed. Morel-Fatio, Geneva, 1885), pars. 311–31.

Greek landlords exploited the fertile estates in the area around Corinth in common with the Franks, dividing the seignorial revenues. The French Chronicle (ed. Longnon, pars. 663 ff.) calls these lands *casaux de parçon*. In the 1290's, in a period of peace between Prince Florent and the Greek emperor, Greek noblemen who owed allegiance to the latter shared the *casaux* with vassals of the prince. One of the emperor's men, however, so abused his rights that the serfs complained to the Franks that they could not endure two seigniors.

[4] On the special position of the English earls and barons—whence derived the peers of the House of Lords—see p. 166, below.

In a case in the High Court of Morea in 1304, involving a daughter of

The grand officers occupied an exalted place in the hierarchy of Morea, being generally chosen from among the leading barons. The offices of the constable and the marshal were as a rule hereditary. Until a remarkably late date as compared with the West, the grand offices were effectively administered by the barons. There is no evolution either in Jerusalem or Morea whereby the office becomes titular in a great family while a subordinate performs its duties. In the West, as administration, finance, and justice became increasingly complex and specialized, a new class of professional administrators, often of non-noble origin, became important and often entered the ranks of the nobility through grants of land or of offices considered as fiefs. This process began earliest in well-centralized states like the counties of Anjou and Flanders, the duchy of Normandy, and the Norman kingdom of England. It hardly got started in the more loosely and simply organized states of the crusading East.

We hear of no seneschal in Morea, although the male Villehardouin princes were seneschals of the Latin Empire. The seneschal was the most important officer of the Capetian kings until Philip Augustus suppressed the dignity in 1191 as being too dangerous to the royal authority. He was likewise the most important officer in the great seigniories of France, having the supreme military, administrative, and judicial authority after the ruler. In Jerusalem he is the highest dignitary in rank but is less important than the constable in practical influence. Several of the functions which the Jerusalemite seneschal alone performed were shared in Morea by three or four officials: thus the chancellor presided over the High Court in place of the prince, the protovestiary and the treasurer were the financial officers, and the purveyor of the castles inspected the fortresses of the principality.

The constable of Morea is appropriately called the "great" or "grand" constable, although this attribute is better deserved by his counterparts in Jerusalem and Antioch, who were clearly the most

---

William de Villehardouin and the Count of Cephalonia, the marshal of the principality objected to the intervention of a "master counselor" of the prince, who was not among the peers. The two litigants are considered as belonging to the twelve baronial peers, "the which must not be judged in court in the company of the other barons and liegemen." (French Chronicle, ed. Longnon, pars. 960–61. On this case cf. further pp. 167–68, below.)

powerful of the officers there, owing to their position as military commanders. The constable in France became significant only after Philip Augustus' suppression of the seneschal's office, but it was not until the fourteenth century that he became the supreme military commander. The marshal derogated from the military authority of the Moreot constable, but the latter was unquestionably the highest civil officer. Jean de Chauderon, in whose family the constableship was hereditary, was temporarily regent of the principality upon the death of William de Villehardouin in 1278 and accomplished several difficult diplomatic and military missions subsequently. Charles I of Anjou rewarded him for his military and political services with the title of admiral of the kingdom of Naples.

The hereditary marshal of Morea not only commanded the prince's troops but also was the supreme military judge—here, too, he exercised a function reserved to the constable in Jerusalem. Jean I and II de Neuilly, barons of Passavant, were the first two marshals of Morea, and so completely was the hereditary character of the office recognized that on the death of Jean II his daughter Marguerite inherited the dignity and through her marriage to Jean de St. Omer brought it to the powerful Theban family.

The Moreot chancellors known to us were not churchmen as in the West and the older crusading states. But like their counterparts elsewhere they did more than act as the chief secretaries of their rulers. The chancellor of William de Villehardouin, Leonardo, who came from Veroli in the Papal States and became a large landholder in Morea, was an intimate counselor of the prince, and presided over the High Court when the prince was himself a party to a lawsuit before it. Thanks to his own abilities and to his relationship by marriage to Charles I of Anjou, Leonardo played an important role in the negotiations which attached the principality to the house of Anjou and involved its fortunes in the Angevin plans to conquer the Byzantine Empire.

The leading financial officer of Morea was the protovestiary, who may also be ranked among the grand officers. The title was borrowed from the Byzantine administration, where it referred to the keeper of the imperial wardrobe and the privy purse—functions that were performed by the chamberlain in feudal states in the

West. The Assizes of Romania (art. 171) refer to the financial duties of the protovestiary: he is the official who farms out the revenues of the prince. He also was well informed on the extent and location of the prince's fiefs, for we learn that the suzerain consulted him in making new grants, and that he acted for the latter in putting the grantee in actual possesion.[5]

We find no trace of a butler among the officers of feudal Achaia, and while the office existed in Jerusalem and Antioch it was clearly of minor importance. The castellan was the most important local official in Morea, and in the case of the two important castellanies of the prince's demesne the castellans were sometimes barons of the first rank.[6] The castellan administered the rural area around the castle and whatever towns were within his district. Among his western counterparts are the Norman viscounts, the English sheriffs, and the Flemish *baillis* and castellans. The Moreot castellan was assisted by a constable and sergeants.[7]

One other distinct group has a place in the feudal hierarchy—the archbishops, bishops, and abbots, who made up the higher secular and regular clergy. The clergy as a whole, of all ranks, was a privileged class. In particular, the special spiritual jurisdiction to which clerics were subject set them apart from laymen.[8] How-

[5] French Chronicle (ed. Longnon), pars. 526, 752; Greek Chronicle (ed. Schmitt, l. 7680–81. A document of 1283 tells of the appointment of a Riccardo de Pando de Scala as "chamberlain or protovestiary of the Principality of Achaia and of all the land of Morea" by Charles, Prince of Salerno and Vicar of the kingdom of Naples (the future Charles II). Riccardo's duties as manager of the royal farms and vineyards and as paymaster of Angevin civil and military personnel are described in detail. He is at the same time appointed master of the royal mint at Glarentza, where he will continue to coin the small *tournois* (cf. Assizes, art. 204). (Camillo Minieri Riccio, *Saggio di codice diplomatico* . . . [2 vols. in 3, with Supplement, Naples, 1878–83], I, 204–5.) Under the Angevins, especially in the fourteenth century, the office of protovestiary was at times held by Greeks, who naturally were in a better position than the Angevin functionaries to know the condition of the prince's demesne, the exact terms on which his peasants held their fields, etc. See especially the documents recording grants to Niccolò Acciaiuoli by Catherine of Valois and her son Robert in 1336 and 1337, published in J. A. Buchon, *Nouvelles recherches historiques sur la principauté française de Morée* . . . (2 vols., Paris, 1843), II, 51–65, 71 ff.

[6] See further on the castellanies, p. 168 and n. 18, below.

[7] French Chronicle (ed. Longnon), pars. 543, 753, 854; Greek Chronicle (ed. Schmitt), l. 8297.

[8] See further p. 175, below. Socially speaking the clergy can hardly be re-

ever, it was the higher clergy alone who were properly members of the feudal class, as administrators of vast properties that had been brought under the scheme of feudal tenure. In the early feudal age it was the rule rather than the exception for prelates to serve personally for their fiefs, despite the canon that forbade clerics from taking human life or shedding blood. Leo IX (1048–54), who began the great series of reform papacies of the eleventh century, had himself been an excellent commander who owed his appointment as bishop of Toul mainly to his military abilities.

Bishops and abbots had their own vassals, making grants in the name of their churches and convents, and often exercised extensive powers of government and justice, which in many cases went back to the charters of "immunity" expressly granted by the Carolingian monarchs to estates of the Church.[9] The popes themselves were not only seigniors of the Papal States of central Italy but also made use of the vassalic relationship to bind several states in alliance to the Holy See, notably the Norman kingdom of southern Italy.

The high churchman in feudal society had to be much more than a priest: he must be political leader and counselor of his lord as well, and often a warrior. It was inevitable that lay lords should try to control the appointment of bishops and abbots, so as to have the kind of vassals they wanted. That such appointees might be objectionable to the Church from the spiritual point of view was a secondary matter to the seigniors. By the second half of the eleventh century lay control of the Church had become alarmingly complete: lay lords controlled the nomination of bishops, abbots, and priests; they invested the higher clergy with their fiefs and received their homage; and they even bestowed the symbols of their holy office upon them, such as the crozier and the ring in the case of the bishops. The great reform movement inaugurated by Leo IX and vigorously continued by Gregory VII (1073–85) brought about desirable changes of form but did not seriously affect lay con-

---

garded as a distinct class since men of diverse origin, education and power belonged to the clerical order.

[9] For an excellent picture of an ecclesiastical fief and of the dual status of its holder as bishop and lord see S. E. Gleason, *An Ecclesiastical Barony of the Middle Ages: the Bishopric of Bayeux, 1066–1204* (Cambridge, 1936).

trol of church appointments. Prelates henceforth were to receive the symbols of their office from other ecclesiastics while continuing to be invested with their fiefs by the lay suzerain. Another reform, only partly successful, was the substitution of an oath of fealty for the more binding engagement of homage. Personal service by clerical vassals was exceptional in the twelfth and thirteenth centuries: through subinfeudation or hire substitutes were readily found. All sorts of church property and revenues, especially abbeys, parish churches, and tithes, were illegally held as fiefs by laymen. Sometimes bishops themselves had given abbeys as fiefs to laymen, or abbeys voluntarily became vassals of neighboring lords. The Cluniac and Gregorian reforms began the gradual process whereby much of this property was restored to the Church. Ecclesiastical tithes, which were most widely infeudated, remained so the longest, and were subject to all manner of subinfeudations. Monasteries recovered a considerable number of tithes that had been pledged for money loans.

Feudal practice had so far influenced the church hierarchy that in some cases bishops exacted homage from abbots of their dioceses and from diocesan officials like the treasurer or chancellor, whose offices were held as fiefs. Likewise cathedral canons with rich livings required the homage of canons less well endowed. This abuse, too, was measurably reduced by the Gregorian reform.

THE FEUDAL CONTRACT

The two chapters from John d'Ibelin which comprise article 3 of the Assizes of Romania are a justly famous discussion of the subjects of homage and fealty and especially the mutual obligations of lord and vassal. The ideal more than the practice is described, but as such it is as much the ideal of Morea as of Jerusalem or the West. Ibelin writes in the thirteenth century, though in a society where the relations of a vassal with his immediate or "natural" lord still counted for much. We may expect in a later writer to find a rather specific description of the obligations of lord and vassal. Our oldest sources speak simply of the vassal's duty to "serve" and "aid" his lord, and of the latter's obligation to "protect" his vassal. There was no need to define these obligations at a time when they were very real and virtually unlimited. With definition comes limitation of the feudal contract, especially as regards the vassal's obligations. Far from being required to aid his lord on all occasions, the vassal is told how not to harm him. Already in 1020 we find the feudal contract defined largely in terms of a series of negative commandments, in the famous letter of Fulbert, bishop of Chartres, to Duke William V of Aquitaine.[1] When swearing fealty, Fulbert writes, the vassal should have six expressions in mind: "safe and sound"—that is, he must do his leader no bodily harm; "secure"—he must not endanger the lord's security by giving up his fortified places; "honorable"—he must not injure the lord's rights of justice or other prerogatives; "useful"—he must not injure the lord in his possessions; "accommodating" and "possible"—he must not make it difficult for the lord to do something good, and to accomplish something well within the realm of possibility.

But it is in doing positive good, Fulbert goes on, that the vassal merits his fief. He must faithfully give aid and counsel to his lord. The latter for his part must do unto his vassal as he would have his vassal do unto him. Both Fulbert and Ibelin emphasize the reciprocal character of the feudal contract; "this reciprocity in obligations that were unequal was the truly distinctive trait of the European feudal class" (Bloch). That the vassal's obligations were heavier, that the vassal owed the lord a certain submission and reverence, is still emphasized by Ibelin as well as by his contemporaries, Bracton and Beaumanoir. The lord does not ordinarily bind himself by an oral or written engagement, as does the vassal. But he is expected to show great respect for his side of the agreement: there is perfect mutuality of fealty, despite the inequality of duties and services. We have already pointed out that the kiss of the homage ceremony signified the social equality of the principals.

Fulbert summed up with the words "aid" (*auxilium*) and "counsel" (*consilium*) all of the positive obligations of the vassal. The most important form which *auxilium* took was that of mounted military service, which we have already described. But *auxilium* might also be financial: in theory the vassal must aid his lord with

[1] Text in *Recueil des historiens des Gaules et de la France, X,* (Paris, 1874), 463; translated in E. P. Cheyney, *Translations and Reprints from the Original Sources of European History* (Philadelphia, 1898) IV, No. 3, p. 23.

his purse whenever the latter found himself in straits. The occasions and the amount of payment varied greatly, but four "aids" came to be distinguished as regular in many parts of the feudal world: for the ransom of the lord when captured; for helping the lord pay the expenses of marrying his daughters and knighting his sons; and for the expense incurred by the lord when he armed himself to go on the crusade. The obligation was onerous, often being the equivalent of the annual income of the fief, and it became universal practice for vassals to pass on the burden to lower tenants and eventually to the villains and serfs. Some of the occasions might be strictly defined: in northern France and England it became customary to give an aid for the knighting of the lord's eldest son alone and for the first marriage of his eldest daughter. Morea seems to have had only two aids, ransom and marriage. In Jerusalem we hear only of ransom. But this was a most important obligation in military states like Jerusalem and Morea. Not only must the vassal serve as hostage for the lord during the raising of the ransom (art. 15), but he must also, in Jerusalem, sell the fief of his wife to help raise the ransom of the king when captive; such a fief, however, was one which was expected to escheat to the king for lack of heirs.

Other pecuniary obligations of the vassal included inheritance-relief (described below as an "incident") and the payment of purveyance, which represented the commutation into a fixed sum of the expense of boarding the lord and his retinue when they visited the vassal on his manor.

Giving counsel, or "service of court," was the most important obligation after military service. The vassal must without fail answer his lord's summons to appear at his court, usually on the important feast days, Christmas, Easter, and Pentecost. We must understand "court" in a broad sense—it consisted of the lord and his vassals, meeting either in a judicial capacity, or as a political council, or on social and ceremonial occasions. When the court functioned as a judicial tribunal, the vassal sat with his peers and judged cases involving the peers in relation to their lord or to one another (cf. Assizes, art. 8). As a council the court gave advice or "counsel" to the lord on any important questions affecting the seigniory. The court was the highest judicial and administrative organ of a fief. On the "national" level, as in France and England, the *curia regis,* or court of the king as the highest feudatory, considered itself competent to deal with all questions—whether judicial, financial, administrative, military, or ecclesiastical. It is in the Anglo-Norman feudal state, starting in the twelfth century, that we can best study the process whereby the *curia regis* became differentiated or specialized into separate departments of finance, justice, and so on, with a trained professional personnel that superseded the unlettered feudal nobles.

Finally, the feudal court, small or large, fulfilled a variety of functions which were outwardly social and ceremonial but often possessed political significance. The lord would choose an assembly of his vassals as the occasion to distribute gifts of horses and arms, or to create new knights. In general, service of court, by bringing lord and vassal into frequent contact, helped to renew the force of the vassalic tie, especially in the case of vassals living on distant fiefs.

The positive obligations of the lord toward the vassal are readily summarized. He must obviously provide protection and defense of the vassal's person and of his fief "against all men who can live and die." This protection might take the form of military aid (Assizes, art. 16) or of legal support in a superior court if a claim were brought against the fief (art. 12). In article 3 Ibelin commits the lord to aid his vassal on two specific occasions: to secure his release if he has served as a hostage for his ransom (cf. also art. 15), and to compensate him if he has served as a pledge with his fief and suffered economic loss.

In the case of conflict between the lord and his vassal, the lord cannot decide the issue arbitrarily, but must see justice done by the vassal's own peers. There is no point of the public law of the crusading foundations that is more characteristic than this provision, or more strongly insisted upon (cf. Assizes, 4, 6, 9).[2]

In addition to these obligations, it is convenient to classify at this point the rights which a lord enjoyed to several forms of income. These are often called "incidents" because they were occasional rather than regular sources of profit.

[2] For further remarks on trial by peers, see the section on justice, below, pp. 165 ff.

I. Relief

When a vassal died, his heir—the eldest son whenever possible—paid to the lord a sum known as "relief." Only then would the lord invest the new vassal with his father's fief. The custom reminds us that in the early feudal period fiefs were held "precariously" as grants of land revocable at the lord's will or returnable to him upon the grantee's death; their transmission from father to son was not unquestioned. The sums paid as relief were substantial. One year's profit of the fief was the ordinary amount of inheritance-relief in the West. In England in the twelfth century it was often (but by no means always) fixed at 100 s. for a knight's fee, but a baron or earl was left to bargain with the Crown to fix the amount. Excessive reliefs were a main grievance of the revolting barons in 1215; Magna Carta specified the amounts for knights' fees (100s.) and baronies (£100). Article 34 of the Assizes of Romania does not specify any amount, although article 31 fixes the amount of the "marriage-relief" paid by the widowed liegewoman who remarries at one-third the annual revenue. We may summarize article 34 as follows: all heirs, male and female, pay relief except (1) the son, when he inherits a *paternal* fief; (2) the ward, when he comes of age; and (3) the liege vassal, for a holding by simple homage. In England and Normandy all heirs paid relief whether direct or indirect descendants of the deceased. In France by the thirteenth century it was commonly paid only by collateral heirs. The custom was least observed in German feudalism. Exacting relief from the ward at his majority was a species of extortion practised by unscrupulous lords. Chapter 3 of Magna Carta prohibits the king from taking relief from wards for whom he has been guardian.

Smaller sums, or some sort of special service, were also often rendered by the vassal when the lord died and a new lord entered into possession of his estates. This "lesser relief" was current in England in the twelfth century as well as in many other feudal states, but it was never as regular as the greater relief paid when the new vassal did homage.

"Relief" (*relief* or *rachat* in French) was not merely an inheritance due; as article 34 attests, it might be exacted on many occasions when a fief changed hands. Unlike Morea, in France collateral relatives who served as guardians usually paid a relief. When the Moreot liegewoman paid a relief upon remarrying (art. 31) it was not in order to purchase permission to marry but rather to buy from the lord the right of taking her fief to her husband, a new holder. Such a *rachat* was paid to the Count of Champagne in his demesne land at Troyes, where it amounted to the entire annual revenue of the fief. It is possible that Champenoise custom directly influenced the law of Morea, for the Villehardouins came from Champagne, and the payment of a relief to remarry seems not to have been a widespread custom. The many kinds of relief exacted from women according to article 34 suggests that they were constantly acquiring real property in various ways and that in a society like feudalism, so completely dominated by the male, the weaker sex must be amerced, as it were, for its acquisitions. The chronicle sources amply attest the constant warfare and heavy loss of fighting men in Morea, especially after 1262.

II. Escheat

When the holder of a fief dies without heirs, his land escheats, or reverts to the lord. The latter, whose rights to the fief had never ceased, now assumes full control and may regrant the fief or add it to his demesne. But as article 104 of the Assizes makes clear, he must not increase the obligations of the vassals of the escheated fief, that is, of his recent sub-vassals. This is a characteristic provision of feudal codes. Under Henry II of England the tenant of a barony that had escheated to the Crown was differentiated from the tenant of a fief that had always held of the Crown. The tenant "of the escheat" continued to pay the customary relief and need not attend the Curia Regis, remaining a member of the court of the escheated fief. King John ignored the distinction, and exacted increased obligations and services from such tenants: hence his promise in Magna Carta (chap. 43) to observe the distinction.

Must there be a failure of all heirs, direct and indirect, for escheat to take place? Generally speaking, yes, in Morea as in the West. But as late as the eleventh century in France the lord frequently claimed an escheat when direct heirs were lacking, ignoring the claims of collateral heirs. And what if the only direct heir were a bastard? In most cases he could not inherit, but the exceptions were numerous enough, especially in great fiefs. By the thirteenth century in France and Germany the influence of the clergy had succeeded in disqualifying the bastard as an heir and in general weakening his legal capacity. In England he fared rather better, but this may well have been "due to no deeper cause than the subjection of England to kings who proudly traced their descent from a mighty bastard" (Pollock and Maitland).

III. Forfeiture

Forfeiture refers to the act of depriving a vassal of his feudal land for serious cause. Such cause might be any breach of the solemn tie that binds lord and vassal. The Assizes mention "homicide," "treason," and non-performance of service as breaches which result in disinheritance upon trial and conviction (art. 69). Desertion of one's lord in battle is a specific treasonable act cited in article 167. The most common felonies or breaches of the feudal tie were the refusal to do homage and the withholding of military service. Since confiscation was a drastic measure, the lord was careful to summon the offending vassal to his court to be judged by his peers. Frequently the vassal refused to appear and defied the lord in the latter's attempt to carry out a sentence of confiscation. The result was "private" warfare between lord and vassal to settle the issue. Often enough in France in the twelfth and thirteenth centuries, where cases of breach of loyalty were very numerous, various settlements short of real confiscation and disinheritance were made. In contemporary England, where royal justice rapidly encroached on baronial courts, the ordinary vassal could not readily be dislodged from his fief merely for refusing to do service. The lord might seize the land by a judgment in his court but "only as a mere gage . . . and as a mode of coercing the tenant into the path of duty. He may take no fruits from the land, he may make no profit of it. . . ." (Pollock and Maitland). The Moreot lord, however, according to article 24, may keep the service of the serfs for himself, may appropriate part of the produce after forty days, and finally obtains the fief after a year and day.

Morea has an interesting case of forfeiture involving the powerful baron of Karytaina, Geoffrey de Bruyères, who was the nephew of Prince William. Early in the 1260's Geoffrey went to Apulia with the wife of one of his liege vassals. According to the Chronicle of Morea, Manfred, King of the Two Sicilies, strongly reproached him, both for abandoning his liege lord Prince William in the latter's struggle against the Greeks of Constantinople and for his illicit relations with the wife of his own vassal. He ordered him to return at once to Morea to seek his lord's forgiveness for his double breach of fealty. Geoffrey made humble submission before William and his court, and on the strong pleas of the leading prelates and knights, the prince forgave his errant vassal, regranting his forfeit barony to him as a "new gift" to be held only by Geoffrey and the heirs of his body. The fact was, as William's councillors (and Geoffrey's peers) pointed out, that Geoffrey was an invaluable military ally whose services must excuse even his unpardonable felonies. Thus practical politics never ceased influencing the theoretical regulations of feudalism. We are not told what, if any, penalty was imposed on Geoffrey for his violation of the sanctity of his vassal's household.

NOTE ON HOMICIDE AND TREASON

Undoubtedly "homicide" (*homicidio*) as used in the Assizes of Romania is criminal homicide, probably the Venetian compiler's translation of the medieval French *meurtre,* with its usual meaning of wilful and "concealed" slaying. "Treason" is a term of changing meaning into which it is easy, and often very misleading, to read modern meanings. Throughout the feudal world, West and East, it meant in theory any breach of the loyalty which the vassal owed to his lord. While the Assizes do not define any treasonable acts, we may be sure that desertion of one's lord in battle was treasonable (art. 167). In the interpolation from John d'Ibelin (art. 3), among the vassals's obligations of fealty there are several whose infraction was generally regarded as treasonable—like bearing arms against the lord, adultery with his wife, violation of his daughter, and refusal to serve as hostage for him or to rescue him in battle. In the much fuller Assizes of Jerusalem we can trace the evolution of a law of treason culminating in Ibelin's discussion of specific crimes that were considered "treason apparent" in the thirteenth century. But neither in Jerusalem nor in Morea was there any concept of treason as the crime of *lèse majesté*, as the plotting or "imagining" of the death of king or lord. Treason had to be done, the harmful result must have been accomplished, for the law to take notice.

Article 18 makes the important point that a man's legal capacity is not damaged while he is merely suspected (however strongly), or remains unconvicted, of a crime, even one so serious as treason. In the historical case cited the accused died a natural death before he was convicted, and was succeeded by his heirs in the usual fashion. The history of France and England provides numerous examples of accused traitors who chose to die under torture, without confessing, and thus saved their property to their heirs. We must assume that death, probably by hanging, was the punishment inflicted on those convicted of murder or treason, and that their property was permanently forfeited to their lords, with attainder of the heirs of traitors. While a convicted murderer could will his personal property (art. 167), the convicted traitor could not. England is not nearly so lenient: an accidental murderer not only must secure the king's pardon but also forfeits his movables.

IV. Wardship

Wardship was the right of the lord to take control of a fief and enjoy its revenues when his vassal died leaving only a minor heir. The lord supported the heir in a manner befitting his social rank until he reached his majority and received the investiture of the fief. Wardship thus involved a kind of temporary escheat of the fief to the lord during the period that the minor could not do military service and perform the other duties of a vassal. Although seignorial wardship was characteristic of all feudal societies in their early period, it persisted unchanged chiefly in Normandy and England while giving way in France and the crusading East to the hereditary principle. Thus in Morea either parent of the ward may serve as guardian, or, if both parents are dead, the nearest collateral relative does. The lord is guardian only when he happens to be heir. It is interesting to see that seignorial wardship is the case in Antioch; we need hardly doubt a Norman influence here. Jerusalem seems to have had the wisest arrangment: the next heir after the minor would receive custody of the lands, while a relative not in line of succession would receive the custody of the child's person. As Pollock and Maitland put it, "to commit the care of a child to the custody of his expectant heir was to set the wolf to guard the lamb." The more prudent arrangement of Jerusalem was in effect at times when the king was a minor; Baldwin IV (1174–85) and Baldwin V (1185–86) are the best-known examples. Despite safeguards the institution of wardship was exploited by guardians, whether lord or relative. It is not surprising to find a provision against the abuses of wardship in the Assizes (art. 83). No doubt the most famous provisions of this sort are chapters four, five, and thirty-seven of Magna Carta, which sought to reform abuses in the practice of wardship by King John. A celebrated case in which an accounting was demanded by an heir of his former guardian in the crusader states arose when King Hugh I of Cyprus (1208–19) accused Walter de Montbéliard of bodily cruelty and dissipation of the royal treasury, and summoned him to render an accounting before the court. Walter fled to Syria instead of facing trial, so that the case had not too satisfying a conclusion.

The Assizes of Romania treat wardship relatively fully and clearly. Article 218 is unique in the entire code: the compiler actually defines a term, "guardian." A group of articles (54, 85, 103) throws light on the ward's status. He can be invested at the age of fourteen; but he does not get seizin—that is, full possession—of his inheritance until he is a year older. The female ward may be invested upon beginning her twelfth year and takes possession a year later. The investiture of a ward before his majority seems to be an act of accommodation by the lord to enable the ward to do certain things that may be highly useful to him and yet do not affect the status of the land itself. This arrangement appears eminently sensible: thus a ward of an important family might conclude a highly desirable marriage through his ability to dower an heiress before attaining his majority. But a true alienation he cannot make. The invested ward's legal capacity with respect to movables and contracts is remarkably extensive—he "can act in these matters just as if he had completed twenty-five years." In the West the majority of the male heir varied between the ages of fourteen and twenty-one; of the noble heiress usually between eleven and fifteen. In England the age of twenty-one, at first the law of the feudal class only, eventually becomes the common law. Antioch and Jerusalem agree with Morea on fifteen years as full age. We must assume that the ceremony of knighthood took place when the Moreot noble reached his majority. The military exigencies of the crusading states may be the simple explanation of their early majority, though we may not rule out entirely other factors like the earlier maturing of Mediterranean peoples or the influence of specific French customs.

V. Marriage

Closely connected with the incident of wardship is that of marriage. It was obviously to the interest of the lord to have a voice in any marriage the ward might contract, especially in the choice of husband for the female ward. The lord's control of the matter was more complete if he, rather than a relative, was the guardian. More generally, the incident of marriage was the lord's right to be consulted in the marriage of any heiress, whether ward or not, and of widowed female vassals. It was a universal precaution in feudal society that no woman should marry an enemy of her lord. In Morea the vassals of liege rank could arrange matches for their daughters without formal permission of the lord (art. 80). The widowed liegewoman can freely choose a new husband who is not an enemy, upon payment of a relief (31). The woman of simple homage requires her lord's permission, but cannot in any case be forced to marry. In other states, especially England and Normandy, the lord had a closer control of marriages of heiresses and widows. In Jerusalem the widowed liegewoman must marry at the end of the first year of her widowhood and must choose from among three candidates selected for her by the lord. Refusal to choose on this occasion, or remarriage without the lord's consent at any time, resulted in the forfeiture of her fief. In England during the reign of John, wealthy widows had to pay considerable sums to obtain charters permitting them to remain unmarried. Chapter eight was inserted into Magna Carta to prohibit this method of extortion; but widows, when they did wish to marry, had still to obtain the consent of the crown or other lord.

VI. Breaking the Feudal Contract

Failure on the part of lord or vassal to observe the terms of the feudal contract had serious consequences. If the vassal were the defaulting party, the usual penalty was confiscation of his fief. The Assizes of Romania list the following causes of confiscation: desertion of the lord in battle (167), homicide, treason, and nonperformance of service (69, 24, 51). Article 24 describes the procedure for applying sanctions against the defaulting vassal. Even if the extreme measure of confiscation has to be applied, it does not really go into effect if the vassal's heir offers the required service. This testifies to the complete acceptance of hereditary succession in the law of fiefs in the Latin Orient. In early feudal times in the West confiscation was definitive: the felon's heirs lost their "rights," and the lord either kept the fief or regranted it to a new follower.

Among the earliest assizes of the first kingdom of Jerusalem is the "assize of default of service," cited by Philip de Novare (chap. lxxxiii). It records that the vassal who failed to answer the regular summons to service lost his fief for a year and a day, once his absence was certified in court. The loss might be for life if the summons had occurred in a time of pressing danger, presumably an attack by the Moslems. Neither in Morea nor in Jerusalem did the lord adopt a measure as serious as confiscation without summoning to his court the peers of the defaulting vassal.

If it is the lord who is the defaulting party, the aggrieved liege vassal must first, according to the Assizes of Romania (art. 7), seek justice in the lord's court. This measure failing, he can transfer his homage to the lord of his lord and seek justice and protection from the higher lord. While this action is the main recourse of the aggrieved vassal in both East and West, the law of Morea provides that the vassal can take the extraordinary step of summoning his peers and together with them withholding all service from the common lord (Assizes, art. 88). In Jerusalem the tenants-in-chief followed the same procedure against *le chief seignor* of the realm. Indeed, even the lesser lords could ask the entire Jerusalemite peerage to default on their service in order to force the king to do justice. This situation was made possible—at least in theory—by the celebrated assize which King Amaury persuaded the High Court to formulate in 1162. By this *assise sur la ligece* rear-vassals of the crown were required to do liege homage to the king alone. The homage to the crown took precedence over any other allegiance and made the rear-vassals peers of the tenants-in-chief. The High Court was open for the protection of the fief of any vassal. While Amaury expected through the assize to win the support of the mass of rear-vassals against the powerful class of tenants-in-chief, in practice it was invoked to justify the collective action of the latter against the crown, especially in the thirteenth century. It was, in fact, regarded as legalizing the revolt of the Jerusalemite or Cypriot barons against their lord, the king.

The feudal legists of the West likewise affirm the right of vassals to coerce the lord and to subject him to the will of his court, but these ideas are nowhere so fully and repeatedly expressed as in the Assizes of Jerusalem, while their practical application in the thirteenth century is a well-attested fact in the Latin states of the Orient.[3]

The *assise sur la ligece* was an unsuccessful attempt of the Jerusalemite crown to "immediatize," that is, to win control over the rear-vassals by eliminating the authority of their direct lords, who stood in a "mediate" relationship to the chief suzerain, the king. In the West a strong tendency toward immediatization showed itself from an early date. For a variety of reasons the higher lords were desirous of becoming the immediate lords of their sub-vassals, while the latter were interested in transferring their homage to a higher suzerain. Practice belied the famous axiom, *vassallus vassalli mei non est meus vassallus.*[4] Strictly, this was the only possible relationship. A vassal could enter into the solemn feudal contract with only one man, his immediate or "natural" lord. Joinville reports that when St. Louis was preparing the Crusade in 1248 he asked his barons to swear that they would be loyal to his children if something happened to him on the trip. He asked the same of Joinville; the latter refused, for he "was not his man," being the vassal of the Count of Champagne, who in turn owed homage to the king. The fact remains that both the crown and the great lords

[3] Philip de Novare gives the fullest description of the procedure of collective default of service to coerce the monarch; he cites two important cases as illustrations (chaps. xl and lii—Beugnot, I, 517, 527–28). The same argument and illustrations occur in John d'Ibelin's treatise.

[4] The vassal of my vassal is not my vassal.

of France steadily extended their authority to vassals in lower ranks. The multiplication of liege homages in West and East in the thirteenth century, especially through the grant of money-fiefs, aided the process of immediatization. Thus Joinville himself accepted a money-fief from St. Louis during the Crusade; bound in this way to the monarch, the richest and strongest feudatory in France, he might well place the new allegiance before the traditional loyalty to the count of Champagne.

No prince of Achaia obtained an ascendancy over his tenants-in-chief like that which made it possible for Amaury of Jerusalem to obtain the *assise sur la ligece* from his Court. Various statements in the Assizes of Romania (cf. arts. 12 and 28) show that the rule of *vassallus vassalli mei non est meus vassallus* was actively practised. The close of article 28 suggests that there was no immediatization in Morea on the part of the prince. Even in a "just" war of the prince against his lieges, the rear-vassals must fight with the immediate lords if, at the time they did homage to the latter, they failed to take an oath reserving their fealty to the prince. A parallel from English law will make this point clearer. Pollock and Maitland, in discussing the "national" oath of fealty required by the English kings, point out that the Conqueror had exacted homage as well as fealty from all the tenants of the kingdom. The exaction of homage was "a strong testimony to the force of vassalism. It suggests that an oath is necessary in order to constitute the relation between ruler and subject; it suggests that the mere omission of a saving clause might make it a man's duty to follow his lord even against the king; it makes the relation between king and subject look like a mere copy of the relation between lord and vassal." [5]

COMMENDATION

Article 55 is the first of a series of five articles dealing with commendation of land to the lord when a vassal goes outside of the principality. Article 60 largely repeats article 55, adding that if a vassal should leave without the lord's permission, he who is to inherit his fief can obtain it within a year and day (of the illegal

[5] Pollock and Maitland, *History of English Law,* I, 299–300.

departure, no doubt). Article 82 points out that if the departing vassal is not held to personal service he may remain outside of the country indefinitely, as long as he keeps up the service. But if his lord dies he must return within two years and two days of the lord's death to do homage to the heir. Article 101 presents nothing new, but 111 finally defines several "legitimate causes" for departure, which 55 did not stop to do. These are eminently justifiable: an outside succession, an outside marriage, and a pilgrimage to Jerusalem, Rome, or Compostella.

It is easily understood why the feudal vassal, usually owing military service, must not depart the country for any but a serious cause. The limit of two years and two days in Morea suggests the same limit which was allowed for claiming a fief in person when one fell heir to it while outside the country (cf. article 36). In France commendation of one's fief need not be to the immediate or liege lord. If one had several lords he could choose him whom he considered the best defender of the fief during his absence. In 1120, when Count Fulk of Anjou *le Jeune* was about to go to the Holy Land, he commended his county not to his chief suzerain, the King of France, but to Henry I of England and Normandy, of whom Fulk held the county of Le Mans.

INHERITANCE OF FIEFS

In June of 877 Charles the Bald was preparing to cross the Alps in answer to the urgent summons of Pope John VIII, at a time when Saracen raiders had reached the outskirts of Rome. Supposing one of his vassal-counts died on the distant campaign, leaving a mature son, who might also be in Italy on campaign, or an immature child at home? In the famous capitulary of Quierzy (Kiersy), Charles promised that the estate of the deceased count would be administered in the name of the son by his father's officers, including the bishop of the county.[1] Thus already before the end of the ninth century the practice of the hereditary transmission of fiefs had received the implied recognition of one of the Carolingian kings. The Frankish benefice of the eighth century was clearly a

[1] This was but one of a variety of provisions making up the capitulary, which was generally concerned with the government of Charles's kingdom in his absence.

revocable grant: the holder enjoyed the usufruct of the land in return for providing certain services in a satisfactory manner. By the solemn ceremony of homage and fealty a peculiarly close tie had been established between a lord and his man. Upon the vassal's death this tie was broken and the benefice reverted to the lord. He might regrant it to anyone whom he had reason to believe a brave and loyal vassal. This was often enough the practice in the Carolingian period, and it seems highly logical that the feudal system should insist on the principle of the revocability of fiefs during the holder's lifetime or upon his death. But what more natural desire on the part of a vassal than to wish to assure the succession of his own offspring to his office and landed holdings? From the lord's point of view hereditary transmission was not without its advantages—he was probably well acquainted with the vassal's son, who had been brought up in the warrior code of the Frankish vassals and had been associated with his father in ruling over a sizable fief and its population of peasants. Indeed, the son might already have performed the feudal services in the place of his ailing or incapacitated father. The lord's refusal to accept the son as a vassal in his deceased father's place might create a dangerous enemy—or at least demoralize the other vassals, concerned over the future welfare of their families.

The hereditary transmission or "patrimoniality" of fiefs appears thus to have been an early and irresistible development in feudal society. But instead of quickly undermining that society, it was forced to a long compromise with its two basic elements of vassalage and the fief. A vassal dies, and his son inevitably succeeds him —but not until he has acted within precise limits for claiming his father's fief (Assizes, art. 36), has made the significant payment of relief, has performed homage and fealty to his father's lord, and has received the investiture of the land. If he is a minor the lord will have much to say in arranging his upbringing and the administration of the fief, so that its owed services continue without serious interruption. If the heir is an unmarried daughter, the lord will have a voice in arranging her marriage. In the early feudalism, if the vassal left no heir of his own body, the land often reverted or "escheated" to the lord; as time went on collateral heirs asserted their claims effectively.

The most striking turn which the law of descent took in response to the practical requirements of feudal organization was the celebrated custom of primogeniture—the inheritance of the entire fief by the eldest male child. The fief by its nature tended to be indivisible: from the seignior's point of view its division not only made it more difficult to control as a public office but endangered the regular collection of the military and other services which it owed. The eldest male child was preferred, no doubt because on his father's death he was best qualified in terms of experience and physical maturity to assume the difficult burdens of ruling a fief. But so "unnatural" did it seem to exclude the other sons—not to mention the daughters—from one's patrimony that primogeniture was far from becoming a universal custom on the continent, while the "absolute and uncompromising form of primogeniture which prevails in England belongs, not to feudalism in general, but to a highly centralized feudalism, in which the king has not much to fear from the power of his mightiest vassals, and is strong enough to impose a law that in his eyes has many merits, above all the great merit of simplicity" (Pollock and Maitland). That the custom was determined by the lord's interest and not that of the vassal or eldest son is seen in the fact that when a vassal left several fiefs, each child, male or female, was likely to get a fief, the eldest having only the advantage of the first choice. John d'Ibelin (chap. cxlviii) records this custom for Jerusalem. The great Anglo-Norman barons who held land on both sides of the Channel were often succeeded by one son in England and another in Normandy. Germany showed great resistance to the general acceptance of primogeniture, even on the highest feudal level. While there was no question of a division of the royal inheritance, the crown did not necessarily go to the eldest son, and it was thus in 1169 that Frederick Barbarossa designated his second son, Henry, the future emperor, as crown prince.

In general, primogeniture was more strictly applied to the large seigniories—baronies, counties, and duchies, which were veritable states. In the Orléanais, Anjou and Touraine in the thirteenth century a fief smaller than a barony was divided so that the eldest son received two-thirds of the land, including the ancestral manor house. It was generally recognized that the eldest son had a moral obligation to care for his younger brothers; the result in practice varied greatly according to time and place and individual caprice. Many a younger son preferred a career in the Church to a pittance from his father's estate, or chose to seek his fortune abroad, as in the crusading states, Spain, or the Byzantine Empire. Always of course there remained the possibility that the younger sons would take up arms against their brother to force a more favorable settlement. There was, indeed, one important modification of primogeniture in favor of equality which became fairly widespread, especially in France. By the arrangement known as parage, a fief was divided more or less equally among the heirs, but the eldest alone did homage to the lord and performed the usual services. In the eyes of the lord he remained the representative of the fief as a legal and political unit. Parage was often a happy solution, but rarely for more than a generation. A powerful ruler like the Norman duke could make the custom operate in his interest. But elsewhere in France parage tended to complicate feudal relationships and failed to prevent the division of fiefs.

Patrimoniality also worked in favor of the inheritance of fiefs by women. They were quite rigidly excluded from holding fiefs in early feudalism—obviously homage and the military obligations it imposed were not for them. But many a vassal died without male heirs, and why prevent a daughter's succession when her husband might perform all the feudal duties? What was exceptionally admitted in the tenth century became a general custom by the twelfth; Germany, here as elsewhere, was more conservative. Equal division of the inheritance among sisters was more readily admitted than in the case of brothers, even in states where strict primogeniture prevailed. If feudalism was a predominantly masculine society, in which women rarely played an active role, certainly the mere fact that the inheritance of fiefs often had to be reckoned through a female line gave them a definite importance. The marriage "incident" was one of the rights most prized by feudal lords, its exploitation becoming a fine art in certain states. Countless petty wars were caused by disputes over claims through female heirs, while the greatest conflict of the middle ages, the Hundred

Years' War, had its formal origin, at least, in the claim of Edward III to the French throne, based on the fact that his mother was a Capetian princess.

The Outremer law of inheritance presents interesting confirmation of Western practice. The earliest Jerusalemite custom had a rigid simplicity—since continuous military service was required, the vassal could serve for only one fief and his eldest son was the logical and sole heir, requiring the resources of the entire fief to support his onerous service. But quickly enough, through inheritance, new grants, or purchase, many vassals increased their holdings, and Philip de Novare (chap. lxix) describes an assize belonging to the first kingdom by which a vassal might provide service for an additional fief through a hired soldier. The sons of such a vassal each received a fief, for which they did personal service. Both Novare and Ibelin (chap. cxlviii) agree that if a son and daughter are the only heirs each receives a fief on the death of a vassal who possessed at least two fiefs. This departure from the principle of masculinity was abhorrent to John d'Ibelin, the "Old Lord" of Beirut and uncle of the legist, who is quoted by Novare (chap. lxix) as insisting: "If there is only a son one day old and there are forty daughters, they should have no right: for a daughter cannot be the right heir before a son." If several daughters were heirs, Novare (chap. lxxi) reports that the eldest alone inherited in the early years of the kingdom; undoubtedly female primogeniture was not rigidly applied when the inheritance included more than one fief. We are more fully informed on the "assize of the distaff," which instituted equal succession among female heirs. It was adopted about 1170 under the influence of a French knight, recently arrived in the Holy Land (Novare, chap. lxxii; Ibelin, chap. cl). It applied to fiefs which owed the service of several knights: the daughters each received a portion owing one knight. If the heiresses outnumbered the "services," the division was made on the basis of age, the youngest daughters receiving nothing. However, only the eldest represented the fief as against the lord, and her sisters did homage to her for their portions, "saving" the liege homage of the lord. This was, then, a kind of parage, much like the instances of parage in the West in which younger male "paragers" did homage to the "chief parager." In Jerusalem as in France parage tended to turn the younger paragers into sub-vassals of the original lord of the entire fief. It was in order to stop this undesirable subinfeudation that Philip Augustus ordered the suppression of parage in 1209—the first specific legislation on a point of feudal practice by a Capetian ruler.

The law of Morea on the inheritance of fiefs does not differ in any important respect from that of Western Europe or Jerusalem. Article 32 enumerates the following well-known provisions: primogeniture, female and collateral succession, and preference for the relative of nearer degree even though of the female line. Already in the *Partitio imperii* of 1204, the treaty dividing the Byzantine Empire between Crusaders and Venetians, we find a clear affirmation of the patrimoniality of fiefs: "Let each to whom a fief will be assigned possess it freely and absolutely, from heir to heir, as well in a male as in a female [heir], and they should have full power to do with it what they wish, saving however the right and service of the Emperor and Empire." [2] The complete acceptance of the hereditary principle is implicit in all of the articles on succession in the Assizes of Romania. It is significant that relief—the "inheritance tax" of feudal society—was not collected from the son when he inherited his father's ancestral fief (art. 34). Relief persisted as long as it did in West and East more because of its economic value to feudatories of all ranks than because of the force of the early attitude of the precariousness of the benefice.[3]

ALIENATION OF FEUDAL LAND

The power of the highest feudal suzerain to dispose of his land was without practical limit. Having no superior above him he could alienate without restraint; heirs after him could not annul his

[2] *Feudum vero quod unicuique assignatum fuerit, libere et absolute possidere debeat, de herede in heredem, tam in masculum quam in feminam, et plenam habeant potestatem ad faciendum inde quidquid sue fuerit voluntatis, salvo tamen jure et servitio Imperatoris et Imperii.* From the text of the *Partitio imperii* in G. L. F. Tafel and G. M. Thomas, *Urkunden zur älteren Handels- und Staatsgeschichte der Republik Venedig*, 3 vols. (Venice, 1856–57), I, 447–48.

[3] Parage is not mentioned in the Assizes of Romania. The Assizes of Antioch (chap. vi), besides prescribing male primogeniture, provide that among female heirs the eldest alone inherits, and is obliged to support her sisters and arrange their marriages.

grants. He alone could grant without restriction to institutions like the Church or the communes, whose possession of feudal lands was against the better interests of the feudality. These powers all belonged to the Prince of Achaia and are briefly indicated in article 10. Articles 25 and 96 specify non-feudal elements to whom he can make grants, while at the end of article 142 we read that he can turn feudal land into a bourgeois tenement. But though he may grant without requiring feudal service in return, there is a question—discussed in article 11—whether he can make a grant without even a rental. It would seem that his power to create an alod was questioned.

In this last respect, he appears somewhat inferior to the kings of Jerusalem. But in all others his powers are the same, and indeed, their description in the Assizes is very similar to that in the Assizes of Jerusalem. John d'Ibelin has left a summary but comprehensive statement that cannot be bettered in any other legist (chap. cxli):

The chief lord of the kingdom of Jerusalem can make grants out of the demesne of his seigniory, fief or fiefs as he wishes, with service and without service. And those which he grants with service, he can grant for such a service as he wishes. And those which he grants without service, he can grant as freely as he wishes. And he can grant of his demesne what he wishes, and to whom he wishes, and as freely as he wishes, to church and religious houses and to commune and layman. And he can remit all the service which one owes him, or a part thereof for a fief which one holds of him. And that which the chief lord does respecting the above matters, should be and is firm and established; for he is of his seigniory sole seignior and lord, nor does he hold it of any lord but of God. Nor does he owe to man or woman homage or service, nor any other return, because he can do all the aforesaid things and everyone of them. And anything he does, his heirs cannot and should not recall nor undo, neither by the assize nor the usage of the said kingdom.

Such privileges could be permitted but one high lord in most states, and in Morea the prince alone enjoyed a favored position. Article 30 limits the grants made by lieges to one-third of the fief, and on the condition that the proportionate service is required. In settled feudal societies alienation either by sale, free gift, or subinfeudation was usually restricted. The nature of the restrictions, and their efficacy in application, varied widely, and perhaps the safest generalization on the subject for most areas is the "lax principle" which Pollock and Maitland state—"the tenant may lawfully do anything that does not seriously damage the interests of his lord. He may make reasonable gifts, but not unreasonable." In France in the thirteenth century, alienation, especially by sale or free gift, was quite unrestricted even in respect to obtaining the lord's consent. Yet the lord had some substantial compensations, like his right to a share—usually one-fifth—of the purchase price. Subinfeudation seems to have been more effectively limited.

In the crusading states, almost on a permanent military footing, we should expect restrictions on alienations in the interest of constant and well-supported fighting forces. This appears to be the case in Morea from articles 30, 46, 50, and others. Violations of the restriction of subinfeudation to one-third of the fief brought severe penalties (arts. 46, 50), and men of simple homage had to act strictly within the consent of their lords. In the Assizes of Jerusalem, on the other hand, we encounter a rather unrestricted power of alienation although in the same author, John d'Ibelin, there are conflicting statements on the subject (cf. chaps. cxlii, cxliii, clxxxii, ff.). The great number of money fiefs helped to bring about a situation of free trade in lands and revenues. In Morea the "conquest fief," presumably inherited continuously in the same family, was a privileged holding as compared with the fief that was either acquired or inherited after the conquest of the Principality. Thus, according to article 46, the alienation of an entire fief brought about its forfeit to the lord, while a grant of two-thirds of it caused a loss of one-third to the lord, the grantee receiving one-third and the grantor retaining the ungranted third. But the grant of an entire "conquest fief" (art. 50), although it penalized the grantor for his lifetime, resulted in no forfeit: the grantee retained a third, and the heirs of the grantor inherited the two-thirds that had temporarily reverted to the lord. In other words, except for the delay of one generation, we really have here the legal grant of one-third of a fief described in article 30.

Article 81, together with the beginning of article 133, records the universal custom that the heir must be protected against any dissipation of his inheritance through irrational alienation by the ancestor in a mortal illness. Glanvill has perhaps best expressed this notion, pointing out that there might be an "immoderate dissipation of the inheritance"; but he adds that even such a grant will hold good if consented to and confirmed by the heir.[1] The rest of article 133 states the widely prevalent custom that a vassal's power of disposing of his acquisitions is much greater than that over his inheritance (cf. also the first sentence of art. 40). This distinction is brought out in detail by John d'Ibelin (chap. cxliv): he who has received a fief for himself and his heirs can return it to the grantor, while the heirs are powerless to oppose the act. On the other hand, the nearest heir, even though he has been seized of land granted to his predecessor, cannot give it up to the detriment of his coheirs: it is already a heritage that has entered into the family. We have already seen (Introduction, p. 5) how William de Villehardouin felt that it was easier for him to give up territory he had conquered—his own acquisitions—to Emperor Michael VIII than to give up the inheritance received from his brother and father. He of course had little choice in the matter, but the coincidence of feudal theory and the event no doubt provided a certain justification for his act.

In all probability alienation was also restricted in Morea by the custom of *retrait lignager*, which was universal in continental feudalism and persisted in most parts of France until the Revolution of 1789. By this custom the relatives of an alienator or seller had the right to recover the land by paying the purchase price to the buyer. Similarly, by the custom of *retrait féodal*, the lord could buy back from the purchaser the fief alienated to the latter by a vassal of the lord. English feudal law did not know either *retrait lignager* or *retrait féodal:* here as elsewhere the English law is simpler, the result of bold innovations on the part of the professional justices of the king's courts. The *retrait lignager* [2] reminds us that the early Germanic concept of blood relationship influenced various aspects of the private and public law of medieval feudalism,[3] which was so

[1] Glanvill, ed. Woodbine, bk. VII, chap. 1, p. 97; cited by Pollock and Maitland, II, 328.

[2] Literally, the right of preëmption enjoyed by the "lineage," or "family" in a wide sense.

[3] Cf., for more forcible reminders of this influence, the remarks on criminal law and on the blood feud, in the section "Justice," below.

characteristically a social system based on the tie between man and man, both unrelated by blood.

Injurious to the interests of the feudality was the abridgment of a fief through alienation to the Church, which in turn did not alienate but held in mortmain. It was harmful enough when a fief was sold to a cleric since he as a privileged person escaped several obligations of lay fief-holders; but, as Luchaire aptly puts it, "when the grant is made to a *church*, to a *saint*, a personality without responsibility and immortal, the injury is especially serious, because it is beyond repair." In the generalization of a more recent French writer, the Church worked "effectively, during the middle ages, to remove the seignorial and family fetters whose ancient rights had bound individual possession: alms would have been made impossible, the fire of hell, which the alms extinguished 'like water,' would have burned without remedies, lastly the religious communities would have risked starving to death if so many lords, whose only possession virtually was fiefs, had been prevented from giving up any part of their patrimony to the profit of God and of his saints." [4]

By the twelfth and thirteenth centuries in many parts of Europe, restraints and even prohibitions had been placed on alienations to churches and religious orders. The consent of the suzerain was often required and might be strictly enforced, as when religious establishments which had received or bought lands without his confirmation were obliged to give them up within a year and a day. Eventually, the right of the immediate suzerain to authorize the alienation of a fief ascended to the remoter suzerains and, as in France, to the king himself. In England in 1279 the Statute *De Viris Religiosis* was enacted in an attempt—not marked with great success—to check alienations in mortmain. "No religious persons were to acquire land; if they did, the land was to be forfeited to the lord, and he had a brief term given him for taking advantage of the forfeiture; if he failed to do so, the lord next above him in the feudal scale had a similar opportunity; and so on up to the king" (Pollock and Maitland).

It is hardly surprising to learn of similar restrictions in the Latin states of the East. In the earliest years of the Empire of Constantinople the crusading lords granted land so liberally to the Church

[4] Marc Bloch, *La Société féodale*, I, 321–22.

that Emperor Henry took the drastic step of prohibiting such "bequests" (*ca.* 1207). The measure stood despite the protests of Pope Innocent III, who pointed out that the Latin Church was merely receiving back in this manner the wrongfully secularized lands of the Greek Orthodox Church. In Morea the highest feudatory alone, the prince, could make grants in mortmain, for grants to the Church by others were valid only during the lifetime of the donors. Article 96 of the Moreot Assizes makes it clear that the prince's consent must be secured for all grants made by others, and again these were only to be lifetime gifts. Jerusalem was one of the earliest of all feudal states to prohibit alienations to the Church by gift or sale, as a number of chapters in the Assizes of Jerusalem attest in clear and detailed fashion. According to the *Livre au roi* (chaps. i, xlv) the king himself could neither sell nor grant any fortress of the realm to the Church or a religious order, while no individual could sell his fief to them. The *Livre au roi* reflects late twelfth-century law, and though we should expect the law of the thirteenth century at least to remain as strict on this matter, in keeping with the trend in the West and in Morea, we find instead that John d'Ibelin clearly sanctions alienations by sale or gift, provided that they are made with the lord's consent. Failure to secure this consent gave the lord the right to confiscate the lands without compensation; land sold with his consent he might purchase back within a year and a day from the Church at the original purchase price. (Ibelin, chaps. ccxxxiv *bis,* ccxlix.)

THE FEUDAL DOWER

The Assizes of Romania give a relatively large amount of attention to the feudal dower. The widow of a Moreot vassal supported herself for the remainder of her life from the income of part of her husband's land. She was of course held to whatever services were owed by this land,[1] and on her death her husband's heir came into full enjoyment of it (cf. arts. 121, 137). We find the basic statement on the Moreot dower in article 35. One of its unusual features is that in Morea as in Jerusalem (cf. Ibelin, chap. clxxvii)

[1] Forty days of grace were given her before service was exigible—article 113.

the dower applies to the husband's acquisitions during the marriage as well as to his own inheritance. This is an archaic survival that had disappeared in the West. Except for acquisitions, the dower was taken out of the inherited possessions of the husband at the time of matrimony (cf. arts. 45, 141). Jerusalemite law differed here (Ibelin, chap. ccxx)—the husband's possessions at his death were taken into account—but that of Antioch accords with Moreot practice (*Assises d'Antioche, Haute Cour*, chap. vi).

Antioch and Jerusalem both agree with Morea on the amount of the feudal dower—one-half of the husband's possessions.[2] This was the frequent custom in France, and according to the thirteenth-century legist, Beaumanoir, it was introduced by an ordinance (which has not come down to us) of Philip Augustus in 1214: "And before this establishment of King Philip no woman had a dower outside of that which had been agreed upon at the marriage" (ed. Salmon, chap. xiii, par. 445). The prearranged dower here referred to generally gives way to the customary or legal dower, like that of the Assizes of Romania. That the prearranged dower existed in Morea—and of course excluded the customary dower—is seen from the last part of article 35: the husband invests his wife, presumably at the time of the marriage, with a sum of money which is to serve as her dower, together with her half-share of his acquisitions. A marriage contract might even be made to exclude her from the acquisitions, as well as from his inheritance; in such a case she is endowed with money and movable goods and may claim no part of her husband's lands. The English and Norman dower was one-third; in England in the thirteenth century this was the maximum dower that could be claimed in lands held by military service; but a socager's widow could claim a half.

Dower was a most valuable resource for the widowed woman in feudal society. It was not readily accepted in the feudal customs, since it meant control over feudal land by the "weaker sex," less

[2] Isabelle de la Roche, sister of John I and William, dukes of Athens, received one-half of the great barony of Karytaina in Morea on the death of her husband, Geoffrey de Bruyères, in 1275, "as dower" according to the Greek Chronicle of Morea (l. 7239). Geoffrey had forfeited his barony on account of felony, and had received it back as a "new gift" only for himself and his direct heirs (see above, pp. 132–33); but there was no question that his widow was entitled to half of the fief for her lifetime.

capable than the male sex of discharging the feudal obligations. But the acceptance of female succession involved the acceptance of the dower as well. It is instructive, none the less, that the consent of the lord is often required when a fief is assigned to a dower (cf. Assizes, art. 58), and that many important fiefs and castles could never be burdened with a customary dower. The smaller dower of one-third in England and Normandy is consistent with the more complete acceptance of primogeniture in both states. Not only was the dower a well-established custom in Morea, but we can even observe a certain solicitude for the rights of the widow in several articles of the Assizes (97, 98, 105, 112, 134). Article 97 makes the point that a traitor's widow has every right to her dower. We find a comparable provision in the Jerusalemite lawbook, the *Livre au roi* (chap. xxii). The compiler of the Assizes notes more than one violation of custom in the interest of assuring the widow her dower and even registers a mild protest in each case (98, 105). If there is uncertainty and inconsistency in several points of the Moreot dower law this situation is only typical of feudal private law generally.[3]

"*Au coucher ensemble gagne la femme son douaire*" (cf. art. 35) —this is the rule that characterized feudal law throughout: the marriage must be consummated before the wife can claim her dower.

[3] Dower land could be alienated only with difficulty: this is certainly the import of articles 66 and 76, although the language of art. 76 is far from clear.
May we infer from article 98 that dower is reckoned against the husband's lands at his death rather than at the time of the marriage? It is entirely likely that this sometimes occurred, though the general rule must be that stated in article 35 and repeated in articles 45 and 137. Naturally if the son married while his parents were alive a paternal or maternal fief had partially or wholly to be divested in his favor if he was to dower his wife (40, 58) unless, as article 35 states, he had set aside a sum of money for her use. Article 45 may refer to a case in which the vassal predeceased both his mother (stepmother) and wife; obviously his widowed mother must not be deprived of her dower in favor of the younger widow.
We should probably not expect the Moreot widow to have to pay relief when invested with her dower fief; but this is stipulated in article 34. The contrary is affirmed in Beaumanoir and other French customs, as well as in chapter seven of Magna Carta.
We have already commented on the interest which articles 98, 112 and 134 present for the general subject of feudal grants (above, p. 112).

THE DOT

Besides the dower, whether prearranged or customary, which originated in the possessions of the husband, women of the feudal class often had the additional resource of the marriage portion, or dot, for their widowhood. If the father had not set aside part of his lands to endow his daughter, her brothers were expected to provide for her after his death. By Norman custom a father could not alienate more than one-third of his lands for this purpose. Under English law, with its strict primogeniture, the son was not obliged to provide for his sisters; none the less, the father had the right to bestow a free gift or "frank marriage" on his daughter, and such land was free from the feudal services for three generations. The practice of giving any sizable marriage portions in feudal land was probably very infrequent in Frankish Morea. That marriage portions were given consisting of movable goods (and perhaps of immovable burgess holdings) is clear from articles 38 and 156 of the Assizes of Romania, in both of which there is a question of disposing of non-feudal possessions by will.[1] There is an interesting mention of the dot at the end of article 124. It was a frequent custom in Mediterranean countries, where the influence of Roman law remained strong, for the husband to add to the marriage portion; the dot together with its "increase" constituted a substantial dower comparable to the feudal dower. Doubtless the dot of article 124 consisted in non-feudal goods, and like the feudal dower in land, it must not be used to pay the husband's debts. The wife was thus protected against the consequences of the bad management of her possessions by her husband.

From articles 174 and 194 of the Assizes we must infer that among the Greek serfs and feudatories the marriage portion was the common method of endowing a bride. The problem of creating a dower out of a fief, which is in conflict with the custom of primogeniture and the interests of the lord, does not arise among the natives of Morea, who practise equal division of the entire land and cannot encumber any part of it with dower for the widow; she must have been provided with a dot.

Article 174 presents several points of interest. It clearly shows

[1] There is also brief mention of the dot in article 132.

the origin of the marriage portion among the family of the bride. If the wife predeceases her husband, and the marriage has been childless, her family recovers the dot: we see here the old belief that a marriage is only provisional until children have been born. Barrenness was regarded as just cause for repudiating a wife, as in the famous instance of Charlemagne and the daughter of Desiderius, the Lombard king. But if the husband survives, and his wife had borne him a living child, even though this child had died at once, he gets unquestioned control of the dot. The first part of article 174 parallels much of the first chapter of the portion of the Assizes of Antioch (pp. 44 ff.) relating to the burgess class, where we learn that one man or three women of good reputation must testify to having heard "the voice of the child or its sneeze." This dependence on human memory for such an important "vital statistic" is typical of medieval society, which lacked the modern penchant for written records and the means for keeping them. The chief significance of article 174 is that among the feudal class proper, in all countries, the birth of a living child gave the husband increased rights over his wife's possessions, whether these were in the shape of inherited land, or her marriage portion, or other. The widower who thus gained control of his wife's marriage portion was the beneficiary of a kind of counter-dower. We find this custom in certain provinces of France, among them Normandy, Anjou, and Maine, and also in England, where it is known as tenancy by the curtesy.

THE TESTAMENT IN FEUDAL SOCIETY. INTESTACY

Given the enormous economic and political importance of land in feudal society, it was natural that the disposition of the fief, whether by various methods of alienation effective in one's lifetime, or by formal testament to take effect on one's death, should have been restricted. In regard to wills, feudalism merely reinforced the Germanic attitude that the family had a vital joint interest in the land and must not permit its easy disposition by the testament of an individual. In consequence feudal land passed intestate from ancestor to heir by various customary arrangements; where strict primogeniture prevailed the succession from father to eldest son was "automatic." "Only God can make an heir, not man" —this saying expresses the medieval attitude: one must not interfere with custom by means of a capricious will, bequeathing the land entirely outside of the family. In the south of France, always under the influence of Roman law, wills applying to land are often met, but significantly, in the case of the important fiefs, their holders made wills precisely in order to assure transmission to an eldest son.

When the will begins to become common from the twelfth century on, it is applied preëminently to movable goods, which are far less valuable than land and are by their very nature easily disposed of.[1] The will is at first essentially a religious act by which the testator gives alms and makes certain bequests to assure the salvation of his soul. But it soon became an instrument for disposing of a greater part of the deceased's non-feudal possessions and satisfying various secular obligations.[2]

In the West the right of testament in movables was generally restricted in regions of customary law. From article 37 of the Assizes of Romania it would appear that the freeman of Morea could pretty completely dispose by will of all of his possessions outside of land held for feudal service. Land held by bourgeois or burgess tenure, as were vineyards, could be sold and willed like a movable (art. 142). The disposable goods also included the current produce of feudal land (cf. also 118); in some customs wheat as soon as sown was regarded as a movable. If the testator in Morea can "freely" make a will, could be ignore his family in disposing of his goods? There may have been no notion in Morea of reserving a "legitimate part" of movables for one's family. This seems to be affirmed by the last sentence of article 156: movables may not go to the wife if the husband has left a will.

According to English law, after debts had been paid, movables

[1] Only the free and legitimately born could hold fiefs: article 115 of the Assizes shows that in Morea a bastard could inherit movables but not a fief.

[2] It was a necessary consequence of the concept of the fief that land must not be used to pay a man's debts: if it were, it would be alienated and the feudal services which it owed endangered. Article 124 of the Assizes agrees with chapter 9 of Magna Carta that a debtor's movable goods alone can be used to satisfy his creditors. An exception to this general custom is the sale of fiefs for debts allowed in Jerusalem and attested in one of the assizes of the twelfth-century kingdom (Philip de Novare, chap. xxvii).

were to be left, one-third to the wife, and another third to the children, while the last third, called the "dead's part," the testator could will as he chose, almost always, of course, including provision for the repose of his soul. Leaving a "legitimate part" to one's family seems not to have been practised in Jerusalem, if we judge from the Assizes of the Bourgeois Court; the Assizes of the High Court are all but silent on the subject of testaments.

Article 56 of the Assizes of Romania accords with the ancient Germanic custom, widespread among the feudal customs, that the husband must at least leave to his wife her personal effects. The English common law was stringent: it assured no share of the husband's personalty to the widow. The husband could will it all away from her except for her necessary clothes; the creditors, likewise, can take everything but these. On this last point the law of Morea was certainly as stringent as the common law.

A few characteristic details on the manner of making and upholding wills are furnished by article 149. The presence of two or three witnesses is an all but universal custom (cf. esp. Glanvill, chap. vii, 6). The ambiguity of jurisdiction over testamentary causes—for who can say what exactly is meant by the falsity (*falsia*) and validity (*sia de valore, o non*) of wills?—is a question constantly encountered and discussed in Western customs. The exclusive jurisdiction of ecclesiastical tribunals over cases of pious bequests is generally recognized. Complete jurisdiction over all wills was attained by the English church courts. In Jerusalem the civil jurisdiction held its own rather better than it did in the West (cf. Bourgeois Assizes, chaps. cclxxxiv ff). The testamentary executor is a universal institution in the thirteenth century. In England he is the "church's lever" employed to compel the heir to pay the legacies.

What if a man dies intestate even in respect to his movable goods? The answer is provided in unequivocal fashion in article 38 of the Assizes of Romania. If the deceased has left a wife she alone succeeds to his non-feudal estate.[3] If the mother is no longer living, the children divide equally, and only in the complete absence of collateral heirs may the lord, after a year and a day, use

[3] "No one," the Bourgeois Assizes of Jerusalem declare, "is so right an heir to a dead man as is his wedded wife" (chap. clxxxvi).

the estate to aid the deceased's soul. A married daughter may not share in her intestate father's estate unless she has first returned her dot: the Moreot custom parallels the English hotchpot. In Antioch the goods of the intestate knight went half to the wife and half to the eldest son; if the only survivors were daughters they shared equally (*Assises d'Antioche, Haute Cour*, chap. vi).

There is apparently no horror in Morea, as there is in the West, of a man's dying intestate, thus unrepentant, having made no bequests for the salvation of his soul. When an intestate died in England, frequently a veritable scramble took place among his relatives, the Church, and his lord for the possession and disposition of his goods. To shut out the king himself as a competitor is the purpose of chapter 27 of the Great Charter. The goods of one who died intestate in Normany were forfeited to the duke.

JUSTICE

The feudal seignior was not alone a political and military chief. His power to judge was an equally important expression of his authority over the fief and its population. The tribunal of which he was the presiding officer enabled him to remind his subordinates at frequent intervals of their duties, and was often the means of turning new or tentative usages into permanent obligations. Significantly, the word *justitia* in the sources means not merely the exercise of justice proper but also of rights of a police and administrative nature, like levying duties on merchandise and taxing markets and business transactions. At times, indeed, *justitia* was synonymous with the seignorial powers as a whole. It was especially prized as an economic resource. Fines, court costs, and confiscations made up an indispensable part of the seignior's income. In a word, justice was a valuable private possession, which might be transmitted, divided, or infeudated like other feudal rights.

Seignorial justice was not of the same competence everywhere. Contemporaries distinguished between "high" and "low" justice.[1] The distinctive traits of high justice were (1) jurisdiction over criminal cases, that is, cases which involved the death penalty or

[1] The possessor of high justice may generally be assumed to have low justice as well in his territory.

mutilation; and (2) the trial of civil cases important enough to warrant the use of the judicial duel as the method of proof to decide the case.[2] In the Carolingian empire the court of the count alone had jurisdiction over criminal cases which involved capital punishment or enslavement. But in the tenth and eleventh centuries, while enslavement disappears, high justice as the power to inflict the death penalty becomes the right of a multitude of feudal seigniors, whose courts were far more numerous than the tribunals of the Carolingian counts. The "cutting up" of high justice in a principality of the size of Morea is typical. The original twelve baronies of the conquest, including that of the Villehardouin family, had rights of high justice.[3] Charters from the large English fiefs or "honors" of the twelfth century provide many examples of grants of rights of justice, including criminal jurisdiction over thieves caught in the act, to lords who were only rear-vassals of the crown.[4]

Low justice may in general be defined as the jurisdiction exercised by the fief-holder over his tenants: (1) in matters relating to the land, like rents and dues; (2) in civil cases among the tenants where the duel was not employed; and (3) in misdemeanors of all sorts. Any holder of land, no matter how low in the social scale, so long as still another individual depended on him, might be a judge. Bloch cites the instance of the holder of a modest tenure in villeinage in twelfth-century France who in turn rented his holding to another peasant, and who then obtained from his own lord the

[2] The judicial duel or ordeal of battle was a combat between the two principals in a lawsuit. More often than not, "champions"—who might even be professional pugilists—fought in their place. In strictest theory the loyal vassal was obliged to be champion of his lord if the occasion arose. See further p. 163, n. 12, below.

The phrases "blood justice" and "pleas of the sword" (as in the duchy of Normandy) are synonymous with criminal high justice. Cf. articles 43 and 94 of the Assizes of Romania.

[3] Assizes, art. 94. Cf. art. 151, which provides that a liegeman who has murdered a serf on premeditation is to be tried by the lord having criminal jurisdiction at the place of the homicide.

[4] F. M. Stenton, *The First Century of English Feudalism, 1066–1166* (Oxford, 1932), 99 ff. The earl of Chester granted lands with rights of criminal justice even to household servants like his butler and his cook. They probably did not exercise these rights, but the grants show how completely a powerful feudatory regarded the highest judicial powers as his own, to bestow on whom he pleased.

right to exercise over that peasant, if the rent were not paid, "'justice for that alone and for nothing else.'"[5]

It must not be assumed that judicial authority in feudal Europe was dismembered to the same extreme degree that rights in the land were shared. Even in France, where the "seignorialization" of land and justice went farthest, the influence of the Carolingian system of public courts did not completely disappear. Feudal counts, in succession to Carolingian counts, exercised jurisdiction over proprietors of alods, over religious establishments, and had quasi-judicial powers over markets and public highways. The highest secular rulers—the kings, dukes, and counts—in France and elsewhere, tended to reserve judicial authority, high justice in particular, to themselves. Normandy and Flanders, among other states, are cases in point. There was not, in fact, any necessary connection between the infeudation of land and the enjoyment or concession of rights of justice. German feudalism offers many examples of separate acts of infeudation of the land and of judicial powers in the same territory. "Fief and justice have nothing in common" was the maxim formulated by the lawyers of the *ancien régime* who studied France's feudal organization. In some French fiefs neither the vassals who held them nor their immediate lords exercised any rights of justice; these belonged to still a third lord. Beaumanoir's discussion of justice in the county of Beauvaisis supports the contrary maxim that "fief and justice are both one." It is true that there existed in Beauvaisis in the thirteenth century a rather complete correspondence between fiefs and judicial authority, both high and low, except for cases specifically reserved to the count's court. But the dictum which separates the fief from justice is more generally true, and certainly agrees better with what is known of the origins of feudal courts.[6]

Thus far we have been discussing justice as the judicial aspect of the seignior's general power of command over the fief and its

[5] Marc Bloch, *La société féodale: II, Les classes et le gouvernement des hommes*, p. 130.

[6] Beaumanoir (ed. Salmon), II, No. 1641: all vassals holding of the count have high and low justice, as do those churches "which have held free estates for a long time, without paying any due to anybody." Beaumanoir goes on to comment in the same paragraph: ". . . there are many countries where some have high justice and other persons low justice, and even in Beauvaisis such a thing might occur, by sale, or by exchange, or by grant of the seignior."

population. If we call this justice *seignorial,* we may then apply the term *feudal justice* to the more narrow jurisdiction of the lord over his vassal. This jurisdiction was concerned specifically with the fulfillment of the vassal's obligations and with the terms on which the fief was held; it also concerned disputes over feudal matters between vassals of the same lord. We might even speak of "contractual" justice to distinguish this jurisdiction from the seignorial variety, for any lord with at least one vassal assumed that the feudal contract gave him the right to judge the man who had done homage to him, thus implying subordination, and to whom he had granted a fief.[7] In the county of Hainaut in the Low Countries, as late as the fourteenth century, a landholder without previous vassals, in subinfeudating part of his land, was said thereby to be "making a new court." [8]

The competence of feudal courts did not extend to litigation alone. Even more frequently they exercised a "non-contentious" jurisdiction, which consisted in approving and recording all changes in the status of a fief. These changes of course included such familiar acts as investiture, a subinfeudation or alienation, the constitution of a dower, an escheat, etc. Only a court of vassals could consider these important changes and make a legal record of them, while adhering to a procedure no less solemn and formal than that required in hearing litigation.

The distinction between seignorial and feudal justice is a useful one for modern analysis, but it must not be drawn too sharply or regarded as universally valid. The French feudatory of the eleventh and twelfth centuries was hardly conscious of it when he summoned his vassals to consider a strictly feudal dispute, or when he personally or through a deputy judged a quarrel between non-noble tenants. It frequently happened that the same court of vassals heard non-feudal as well as feudal cases. Until the thirteenth century in France feudal courts with a strictly defined jurisdiction

[7] In Charlemagne's time the vassal was clearly the subject of the king and was justiciable in the public courts. It was during the troubled period of the ninth and tenth centuries that feudal lords acquired judicial authority over their vassals.

The Moreot lord's right of justice over his vassal's fiefs is evidenced in many articles of the Assizes of Romania; cf. 49, 116, and 153.

[8] *facere novam curiam,* from a document of 1342; cited in N. Didier, *Le droit des fiefs dans la coutume de Hainaut au moyen âge* (Paris, 1945), 88–89.

are the exception rather than the rule. In Germany feudal conceptions did not influence the older judicial administration as deeply as in France. In most areas public tribunals (*Landgerichte*) continued the Carolingian courts, enforcing the common law of the several territories (*Landrecht*), in both civil and criminal actions. Their competence corresponds to what we have called seignorial jurisdiction. The law of the fiefs (*Lehnrecht*), on the other hand, was applied in special feudal courts (*Lehngerichte*), which were new creations with a limited jurisdiction. Thus a German vassal who had committed a crime at common law was tried in a public court. In French custom, however, we frequently encounter seigniors—including many who are not among the great territorial princes—exercising criminal jurisdiction over their liege vassals. Ample justification for such power was found in the homage ceremony: in placing his hands in those of the lord the vassal became his justiciable in every way, in life and limb as well as the fief. But in the thirteenth century the officials of the Capetian kings began successfully to enforce the doctrine that the king alone had personal justice over the feudal nobility. An incident from Moreot history illustrates one of the many forms that this problem might take. In 1303 Philip of Savoy, the new prince of Achaia, imprisoned the chancellor of the principality, Benjamin of Kalamata, when the latter refused to give an accounting of the revenues of the princely demesne lands for several years preceding. Whereupon Nicholas III de St. Omer, the powerful marshal of the principality, angrily demanded Benjamin's release, on the ground that he was Philip's liege vassal whom "he could not arrest in any manner, since his fief was his pledge, according to the usages and customs of the country." St. Omer's intervention resulted in Benjamin's release for a sum somewhat smaller than that originally demanded by Philip. The words which the chronicler attributes to St. Omer are much like those of article 5 of the Assizes of Romania, which, however, admits the lord's right to arrest his vassal on the ground of homicide or treason.[9]

Some familiarity with the procedure of feudal courts is essential to an understanding of the practical operation of feudal justice and of the principles—so different from those of our age—which

[9] French Chronicle (ed. Longnon), pars. 857–867.

underlie it. It is instructive to examine the procedure in the courts of an area like the county of Anjou in the eleventh century, before the Capetian kings had begun their work of judicial and political centralization.[10] The fashion in which trials were conducted in Anjou is typical of what went on in many parts of France in this turbulent period. Anjou in its general political condition stood somewhere in between the duchy of Burgundy—badly split up and at times close to dissolution, and the strong county of Flanders —well on its way to centralization.

Let us picture two Angevin feudatories of the eleventh century contesting the possession of feudal land or of some valuable jurisdictional right. They may be lay lords, or, as so often happened, an ecclesiastical establishment holding feudal land in contest with a lay lord. We have to notice first that there was no court in Anjou with a clearly defined competence or with a fixed seat and time of meeting. That of the count was no exception. It met wherever the count happened to be when he decided to hear a case, and its membership was fluid, both in number and in the identity of the personnel.[11] The count's own vassals might or might not take a case before his court. The choice of a court depended on a private agreement of the contesting parties, often preceded by much wrangling and delay. Once an agreement had been reached, the court was notified and the parties appeared before it. Sometimes the judges insisted on a formal promise by the parties that they would accept the judgment. The pleadings then took place, plaintiff and defendant making a full statement of their claim and defense.

The judges could dismiss the plaintiff's claim on the basis of these pleadings if the defendant (1) took an oath, without anyone appearing to contradict him, that he had had peaceful possession of the disputed object or right for a number of years; or (2) produced a charter making good his right; or (3) produced witnesses whose evidence was not impugned. If the defendant failed in these

[10] See especially L. Halphen, "Les institutions judiciaires en France au XIe siècle. Région angévine," *Revue historique*, LXXVII (1901), 279–307. Halphen's account is based exclusively on records of actual lawsuits.

[11] Cf. article 13 of the Assizes of Romania. Throughout the feudal world no more than two or three feudatories, besides the lord, were needed to constitute a court.

tests, the plaintiff was invited to prove his claim, either by charters, by witnesses, or by one of the more strenuous judicial tests, such as the bilateral ordeal of battle (the "judicial duel"), or the unilateral ordeals of water and the hot iron.[12] The victor in the duel, or the litigant who was uninjured in the other ordeals, won the case; he had obtained the "judgment of God." Thus "judgment" in a feudal trial was simply the decision of the judges that one of several methods of proof should be used, while the "trial" was this proof or test itself, a crude appeal to the supernatural. "Judgment" precedes "trial"! The contrast to modern judicial procedure is complete. We must "discard from our thoughts that familiar picture of a trial in which judges and jurymen listen to the evidence that is produced on both sides, weigh testimony against testimony and by degrees make up their minds about the truth" (Pollock and Maitland).

Not all disputes over feudal property were taken to the courts in Anjou or elsewhere in France in the eleventh and twelfth centuries. Adversaries very often resorted to an out-of-court settlement (*concordia*). Feudal rights were so confused and entangled that even the most rational court procedure would have had great difficulty in determining which claimant was wrong. Often a private settlement suggested itself after a court action had been initiated, and especially when an ordeal was about to take place, or had even begun. In many cases the parties are an ecclesiastical establishment and a layman; the latter makes a claim which the clerical side satisfies by compensation in money or kind in return for the formal renunciation of the claim. A charter is drawn up describing the "concord" and bearing the parties' signatures. In a very weak state like Burgundy, where these settlements are very nu-

12 Battle became the favorite method of "proof" in feudal trials in both East and West. It was very popular in Jerusalem and Cyprus. The Bourgeois Court permitted its use in important cases, but battle between nobles and bourgeois was prohibited. It is John d'Ibelin, of all the feudal legists, who has left us the completest description of trial by battle—of the actual combat and its attendant formalities (chaps. ci–ciii, pp. 165–74). In chap. lxxxi (p. 129) he lists the causes for which the duel was the required proof; these include: murder, homicide, and treason, and all disputes of one mark silver or more. Thus all important litigation, whether civil or criminal, was decided in this fashion. There is no development in thirteenth-century Jerusalem and Morea to parallel the changes in procedure in England and France, where royal authority introduced more rational methods of proof, like trial by jury.

merous and the sums usually small, it is no exaggeration to say that the lay lords practised an almost constant petty blackmail at the Church's expense. In several Burgundian cases known to us the religious houses also include advantages of a spiritual kind in the settlements: one case from Cluny of 1107 involved the large sum of 520 pounds, association of the litigant in the monks' prayers, and the assurance of his being received as a monk when he should so desire![13]

Private agreements were also freely used among feudatories to settle disputes of a criminal character. The list of crimes and misdemeanors in Anjou included murder, incendiarism, rape, theft, the violation of cemeteries, and the failure of lord or vassal in his duty. The old Germanic notion persisted into the feudal age—that the injured party or the victim's kin should be compensated, even if the crime were of the gravest, like homicide and murder. A crime was a private wrong, to be avenged by the victim or his kin. If the criminal withheld satisfaction his relatives must pay—their responsibility was equal to his. Let them surrender their kin or force him to compensate the victim if they wished to avoid the blood feud. If the victim sought the help of the judicial authorities, he faced the great initial difficulty of compelling his attacker to appear before a tribunal. He usually found it necessary to solicit the aid of the count or other powerful lay lord, or of the bishop. In return for a gift such a personage would summon the alleged criminal to appear before his own tribunal. Once both parties were before the court, the procedure followed was the same as that in civil suits. If the criminal failed the judicial test assigned to him, his guilt was proved and the court pronounced the penalty, which in Anjou at this time took the form of a fine. But even when a criminal case was settled in a court it was hardly more than a "regularized blood feud." As late as the thirteenth century, in the best-policed states, like Flanders and Normandy, the murderer was not pardoned by the ruler or the court until he had first made a settlement with the relatives of the slain.[14]

[13] F.-L. Ganshof, "Etude sur l'administration de la justice dans la région bourguignonne de la fin du Xe au début du XIIIe siècle," *Revue historique,* CXXXV (1920), 215–16.

[14] The provisions of chapter 20 of the *Livre au Roi* of the Jerusalem Assizes illustrate the importance of the custom of compounding with the relatives of

One point of procedure in feudal courts calls for special comment. It is judgment of peers—the celebrated principle that a fief-holder is to be judged only by his fellow vassals, by men who are legally and socially his equals. He was thus protected against an arbitrary judgment on the part of his lord. In 1037 Emperor Conrad II acknowledged the right of the lesser lords, lay and clerical, in Italy to be tried by their peers in cases liable to result in the loss of their fiefs. The principle became a universal custom in the twelfth and thirteenth centuries, as the frequent statements in continental and English and Outremer law attest. Nowhere, however, was it more insisted upon than in Jerusalem and Morea. Thus it was invoked during the bitter conflict between Emperor Frederick II, as regent of the kingdom of Jerusalem, and the Syrian and Cypriot baronage, led by the great Ibelin house. When Frederick's legate seized Beirut, which was the fief of John d'Ibelin, the "Old Lord," the barons of the High Court of Jerusalem at Acre protested the arbitrary seizure, on the ground that John had been dispossessed without judgment of his peers. This privilege receives repeated and cogent expression in the Assizes of Romania, especially, again, in cases of disseizin (arts. 4, 6, 7, etc.). By far the best-known expression of the privilege is the thirty-ninth chapter of Magna Carta, in which John promises that: "No free man shall be taken and imprisoned, or disseized, or outlawed, or exiled, or in any way destroyed, nor will we go upon him, nor will we send upon him, except by lawful judgment of his peers and by the law of the land."

---

a murdered man, and also show how remarkably privileged a feudal noble was in relation to a bourgeois. A liege knight has killed a bourgeois. If he flees the kingdom the king shall seize his fief and keep it unless he returns within a year and a day and answers the charges in the court. However, if he settles with the victim's relatives and they bring no charges against him, he may go before the king to ask for the fief by judgment of peers since his crime would then be that of having left the country without the king's consent. If the knight has burgess property like vineyards and houses, and returns within a year and a day after the High Court has seized it, he recovers it if the relatives of the dead have not brought charges against him. However, if the slayer does not flee, but denies the crime in court, the relatives may "appeal" him as the murderer and he is obliged to do battle with another knight. If worsted, he is hanged just as dressed, spurs and all, and all of his property is forfeited to the crown. If his opponent is defeated, he is hanged in the same way, and his bourgeois hirers are in the mercy of the king both as to their property and their lives.

Trial by jury, due process of law, and other precious rights of modern Englishmen have been incorrectly read into these famous words. What they largely meant in 1215 was that the vassals of the crown—the earls and the barons—desired to be judged by their peers in all cases, civil or criminal, in which they were involved with the crown. They were attempting to arrest the progress of royal justice whereby professional judges, often of undistinguished social origin, had become the technical peers and real judges of the tenants-in-chief of the king, and were zealously serving his interests. As events proved, the earls and barons succeeded in obtaining judgment of their peers only in the criminal pleas of treason and felony; this was strictly for themselves alone, not for their own vassals or for ordinary freemen.

In Jerusalem and Morea, however, the lieges of the king or prince were always tried by their peers in all cases. In neither state was there any development, as in England and France, whereby royal or princely justice encroached on the justice dispensed in the High Court and in the baronial tribunals. To point out the persistent and effective application of the principle of judgment of peers in the crusading principalities is to emphasize the fact that these states throughout their existence were controlled by a true feudal aristocracy of barons and lesser liegemen. The rulers of Jerusalem and Morea were *primi inter pares* in a strict sense and as much subject to the decisions and control of their High Courts as were any of their liege vassals. These courts remained undifferentiated in function; their regular, non-professional membership performed in a political, executive, or judicial capacity as occasion demanded. The monarch or prince would convoke and preside over the court and announce its decisions; but it was the members of the court, not he, who judged.[15] The prince of Achaia, when he was a party to a case heard before his court, would surrender his baton, symbolizing his presidency, to one of his vassals, and proceed to argue his case before the assembled court (Assizes, article 8). Indeed, the effective application of the rule of judgment of peers implies that the peers composing the court are in fact freely exercising their function as judges.

We must not, of course, exaggerate the protection which the

[15] Cf. especially article 4 of the Assizes; see also art. 207.

forms of procedure afforded the vassal, any more than we should minimize their importance. The circumstances surrounding every feudal trial varied enormously. A powerful and unscrupulous lord could exert great pressure on his judges to decide a case in his favor. But even the most despotic lord found it difficult to dispense with a collective judgment of the court of his vassals.

The lawsuit involving the barony of Akova in Morea, to which article 36 of the Assizes of Romania makes allusion,[16] illustrates these considerations. Prince William won the case through chicanery, but the fact that the court at one point hesitated to judge the matter in his favor no doubt had its influence in inducing him to grant a third of the barony to Marguerite de Passavant. Judgment of Marguerite's peers, even if imperfect, was preferable to arbitrary retention of the fief by the prince without any compensation.

In another lawsuit in the High Court a more venal prince of Morea, Philip of Savoy, was restrained by a powerful vassal from carrying an injustice too far. Another Marguerite, the younger daughter of William de Villehardouin, had brought an action to recover the personal property of her late husband, Count Richard of Cephalonia, from her stepson, John. The latter had bought Philip's support with a heavy bribe. But when he addressed Marguerite in coarse language, he found himself challenged by a member of the court, none other than the hereditary marshal, Nicholas III de St. Omer, "the most puissant and beloved and feared man of the entire country at that time," in the words of the chronicler. When a favorite of Philip's—a knight who did not belong to the native baronage—spoke in John's favor, St. Omer demanded his expulsion from the court. The marshal had on several occasions shown his contempt for the Savoyard prince who had apparently come to Morea only to enrich himself and his entourage, and now for a moment Philip seemed determined to humble the proud marshal. But advisers like the grand constable, the chancellor, and the bishop of Olena pointed out that a "show-down" with St. Omer would only bring evil on the country. Besides, the marshal was justified in talking more boldly than anyone else on two grounds: he was *le plus gentil homme* of the country, being related to kings

[16] See the note to art. 36 for a detailed account of the case.

and emperors, as well as the most powerful feudatory through his lands and feudal connections; further, he was *si larges et cortois et amiables a toute gent.* This is an admirable summary of the qualities and virtues which the feudal nobility held in greatest esteem. Philip took the frank advice and assigned two lords, including the commander of the Temple in Morea, to arbitrate the difference between the litigants.[17]

The Akova case is an excellent example of feudal or contractual justice, while the case of Marguerite de Villehardouin *vs.* Count John is feudal in a looser sense: the litigants are feudatories but the dispute concerns personal property and not the feudal relationship or the fief. It is an important civil dispute. The High Court of Achaia was of course competent to try criminal cases involving the prince's vassals, and disputes of any character involving bourgeois or serfs on his own domain lands. Cases involving such bourgeois or serfs, however, must have seldom reached the High Court. Rather were they dealt with by the castellans or "captains" of the two important castellanies in the princely demesne, who are referred to in article 177 of the Assizes. Their areas of jurisdiction around the castles of Chloumoûtsi and Kalamata included the towns of Glarentza and Androusa, respectively, the former being the chief port of the principality and the residence of numerous bourgeois.[18]

Besides the prince, at least several of the important barons had rights of high justice over their lands, as articles 43 and 94 inform us. Numerous allusions in the Assizes suggest that in turn lords who were lieges of these barons or of the prince had their own courts of low justice for their vassals and serfs (end of 43, 72, 203). It is hardly to be supposed that the competence of these courts was any more clearly defined than in the West (cf. 177). A litigant did not necessarily take his dispute to the court of his immediate lord. Economic motives doubtless led the owners of courts to compete for lawsuits. Even the lowly Moreot serf might take a civil case to

[17] As a result Marguerite obtained a fifth of her husband's movables. (French Chronicle, ed. Longnon, pars. 955–72.)

[18] The importance of the office is indicated by the high rank of some of its holders, like Giorgio Ghisi, lord of Chalandritza and later an Aegean island baron, who is referred to in the French Chronicle (par. 764) as "chapitaines de la chastellanie de Calamate" in 1292.

the lord of his lord, as article 43 states, just after the preceding article affirms that all feudatories, even men of simple homage, are judges of their serfs in civil cases, with no appeal. Article 162 indicates that criminal jurisdiction, in Morea as elsewhere, was less divided than civil.

Several articles of the Assizes of Romania may be cited for the interesting details they provide concerning feudal procedure. Article 144 indicates that a judgment made after sunset is invalid but may be made on a feast day. Article 145 affirms the superiority of feudal custom over the written Roman and canon law, and insists on oral pleadings in the "vulgar tongue," that is, in French, admitting frankly that the lieges are men of little learning. An important feature of Outremer procedure is the duty of giving counsel described in article 146. Like other early systems of jurisprudence, feudal law was tremendously formal, and counsel or advice on the part of the members of the court was almost essential if the litigant was to avoid mistakes of form in pleading which might cost him the case. To forget the exact words of a formula or to make a slip of the tongue was likely to prove fatal. Philip de Novare (chap. lxvi) warns the litigant to claim the safeguard of *retenail* before beginning to plead: he then had the right to repeat an oath or other set formula if he stumbled over it the first time. The counsel is of course far removed from the modern attorney. He resumes his place on the court bench after assisting the litigant; his capacity as a judge has not been affected. The professional pleaders or advocates who are alluded to in articles 145 and 146 are a closer approach to the modern attorney, but they are not true representatives at law. The litigant is still regarded as conducting his own cause before the court, with the aid of one particularly skilled in the rules of pleading.[19]

An important branch of procedure dealt with summonses and with the time allowed for the preparation and conduct of cases. The three successive citations (arts. 148, 160) were a very old custom common to all the Germanic peoples. The delays described in article 160 reflect feudal custom everywhere. If feudal law seems

[19] In the Akova case Nicholas II de St. Omer is the "advocate" who speaks for his sister-in-law Marguerite, while Prince William appoints himself advocate to plead the cause of the High Court (Greek Chronicle, ll. 7521/28/31).

remarkably patient, bad roads and primitive means of travel were at least partly responsible.

The methods of proof mentioned by the Assizes include the oath (91), charters of enfeoffment (90, 91, 139), witnesses (90, 91, 160, 191, 193), and battle (157). We hear nothing of the unilateral ordeals.[20] The testimony of serfs is allowed in cases concerning land (175) but not in criminal suits involving liege vassals (198).

A litigant has the right to ask for a copy of a judgment, sealed by the members of the court (168). He may even have a copy of the testimony produced in the trial (191). But article 158 suggests that the recording of judgments was haphazard in Morea: human witnesses, preferably at least two members of the court of liege status, may have to be relied upon. This was also the case with charters of infeudation, as articles 90 and 91 show. It was characteristic of early feudal society everywhere, and in some places till a late date, to make sparing use of writing for legal purposes, except for wills and documents concerning land.

The application of an oral and formal procedure, with its rudimentary methods of proof, made no unusual intellectual demands on the unlettered feudal nobility. Yet this procedure was subtle and esoteric in its own way, and never more so than in the trials of the High Court of Jerusalem-Cyprus in the thirteenth century. The treatises of Philip de Novare and of John d'Ibelin are primarily manuals of procedure in which these enlightened men in all good faith do not "explain the law so much as the means of getting round it."

A last word on procedure is reserved for appeal. It is a refinement absent in early legal development, which cannot conceive of a dispute being retried before another court, after it has been

[20] There is no reason to believe they were much used, if at all, in feudal Achaia. The Byzantine historian, Acropolites, relates a curious episode involving Michael Palaiologos and the emperor of Nicaea, John Vatatzes (1222–1254). When under suspicion by Vatatzes at one time, Michael was asked to purge himself by the ordeal of the red-hot iron. He answered that he would submit to the ordeal if the metropolitan of Philadelphia would first take the iron into his holy hands and hand it to him. The ecclesiastic declined to take what he called a test of barbarian origin. Michael thereupon received a trial according to the usual Byzantine forms. Trial by battle, however, was accepted among the Byzantines as a nobler custom, less degrading to their sense of superiority as Graeco-Romans. (Georgius Acropolites, *Opera* [ed. A. Heisenberg, 2 vols., Leipsic, 1903], I, pp. 92 ff.)

judged by solemn procedures regarded as infallible, such as the oath or the ordeal, veritable judgments of God. But the dissatisfied feudal litigant could charge the human judges with malevolence or in any case serious error. This was a crude sort of appeal, a personal remedy against the judges. By a well-recognized procedure the litigant would formally accuse them of having made a false judgment (*fausser le jugement*), and proceed at once to do battle with each singly. No legist gives a fuller description of the procedure than John d'Ibelin. Only if the challenger defeated the entire membership of the court in one day was the judgment reversed. If unsuccessful, he was hanged at sundown. If he were careful to challenge only one member of the court, who acknowledged his responsibility for the judgment, he need fight no others.[21] It is not likely that this risky procedure was often resorted to. Instead of the death penalty it became customary in France in the thirteenth century to impose a heavy fine on the litigant or court member defeated in the duel.

True appeal from a lower to a higher tribunal to correct judicial error is described in articles 143 and 196 of the Assizes of Romania. But this system cannot refer to the administration of justice in the baronial courts and the High Court in the thirteenth century. It can only be ascribed to the Angevin rulers of Morea after 1278, who established a system of appeal probably in order to promote the centralization of their miscellaneous Italian and Balkan possessions. The introduction of appeal procedures in France and England in the thirteenth century was due to the growth of royal power and to the examples of the church courts and the revived Roman law. It was perhaps even more the desire to assist the process of centralization under the crown than the desire to correct injustice to individual litigants that led the monarchs to favor appeal. St. Louis prescribed the use of appeal in the royal domains by an ordinance of 1258, which also abolished the duel. The Parlement of Paris became the highest court of appeal, and eventually its au-

[21] Chaps. cx, clxxxvii. There was no question of his challenging the lord of the court: this is another indication that in a feudal court it was the vassals or peers who judged, not the lord who presided. The "appeal" of false judgment was a privilege reserved to the nobles; neither bourgeois nor serfs could use it. Article 163 of the Assizes of Romania refers to a litigant challenging a counsel; whether the duel supervened remains uncertain.

thority to hear appeals covered lawsuits originally heard in the courts of the great seigniors outside the royal domain. Be it noted that the graduated feudal hierarchy, with its courts on each level, lent itself rather naturally to the institution of a system of appeals. This is one of several ways in which the French kings made effective use of feudal institutions to centralize the realm. Monarchy and feudalism as principles of social organization are not necessarily opposed to each other.

It is necessary to consider briefly how the seignior judged his peasants, if only to appreciate better one or two aspects of the judicial code of the nobility. It is too readily assumed that the peasant was always judged by the lord or by his agent. The facts show that in the earlier feudal age he was very often effectively judged by his own fellows. But the tendency was clearly in the direction of judgment by a superior in a manorial court, so that by the thirteenth century the jurists are asserting that judgment of peers is a privilege reserved to the noble class. They similarly reserved trial by battle for the nobility, but numerous examples might be cited of French villains deciding civil disputes in this fashion, as in eleventh-century Anjou. In such cases the lord's task was limited to indicating the judicial test which the parties are to undergo, and receiving either the fine paid by the loser or the indemnity paid by the two parties if they were reconciled as the test was about to take place.

But the main occupation of the lord or his agent was to punish the crimes and misdemeanors of the peasants. The lord takes the initiative in discovering the misdeeds, instead of waiting for a charge brought by the victim or his relatives, as among the nobility. The suspect is summoned, hears the accusation, and either confesses or swears his innocence. The judge may attack the oath and insist on one of the judicial tests. If the suspect fails the test, or refuses to take it, he is condemned and fined, or sometimes given corporal punishment. If he is a villain who cannot pay, he is depressed to the status of a serf—the lord is enriched whatever the outcome.

A system like this was in rare instances fairly administered by an enlightened lord. But the almost inevitable result was for the lord to abuse his authority and pursue his men for every kind of offence, serious, trifling, or even imaginary, in order to collect fines. Judicial authority over peasants was regarded as one more means of exploiting the villain and the serf. "Justice is a great profit"—so ran the medieval maxim. The notion of justice as a public service was foreign to the lord's conception of his office.[22]

A number of references in the Assizes of Romania to the Moreot serfs as justiciables of their lords suggest that they were not merely exploited economically through the judicial system but were also punished by a harsh criminal code.[23] Their rightlessness or unprotectedness in relation to their own lords is indicated by the closing sentence of article 186: the serf wronged by his lord cannot seek justice in the court of the superior lord. The following summary of the servile traits of the Moreot peasant shows how closely his condition resembled that of the rightless serf of England and France. He could neither give his daughter in marriage nor himself contract marriage without his lord's permission (art. 174). The lord succeeded to the entire property of the serf who died without heirs (185). Further, the lord could at any time deprive a serf of his goods, except for the means of bare subsistence (197). This right is comparable to the arbitrary tax, or tallage at will, levied on serfs in the West, where, however, it had become greatly restricted by the thirteenth century. The serf was a mere chattel, part of the equipment of the fief (25, 107, 211). If a liegeman killed a serf by misadventure he needed only to replace the victim to be free of any accusation (151). Such a crime raised only an economic, not a moral problem. The fugitive serf could be reclaimed wherever found—an important mark of serfdom (203). The serf could not testify against a liege in a criminal case (198). However, his testimonial capacity in suits concerning land was far from negligible (175). A female feudatory who married a serf lost both her freedom and her fief for the duration of the marriage (78, 180). What is more remarkable is that the offspring of such a union were likewise servile, a result that had become rare in the West by the thirteenth century. However, a female serf won her freedom when she married a freeman (125). Voluntary enfran-

[22] On the financial character of seignorial justice see especially G. G. Coulton, *The Medieval Village* (Cambridge, 1926), chap. 16.

[23] Articles 42, 43, 151, 162, 177, 187, 206, 219.

chisement of serfs by their lords is mentioned briefly in articles 25 and 139.[24]

We have still to account for the rôle of the Church in feudal justice. Bishops and abbots, aside from their spiritual functions, were also important feudatories with judicial powers over their own vassals and non-feudal dependents. Article 48 of the Assizes of Romania alludes to the Moreot bishop as a baronial peer. Like lay seigniors the ecclesiastical lords might alienate rights of high and low justice in grants to vassals. Despite the canon that clerics could not shed blood or even pronounce a death penalty, monastic establishments in particular, through their lay officials, condemned and hanged many a criminal and clung tenaciously to gallows-rights.[25] Nor did they show repugnance to the hiring of champions to do battle for them in lawsuits in which they were parties.

In France the monasteries which had seignorial justice employed a lay official, called the *avoué,* to preside over the court. His counterpart in German feudalism, the *Vogt,* succeeded in effectively reserving to himself the administration of high justice within the monastic seigniory. The instances are legion in France of lay lords who dominated monastic establishments through naming the abbots and appointing themselves *avoués,* while designating a subordinate to perform the functions of the office. The *avoué* was remunerated for his services in the form of a fief, which he transmitted to his son. In reality he was often the chief exploiter of the monastic peasantry, much more their master than were the monks.[26]

[24] In Morea as elsewhere the "letter" or charter of enfranchisement (cf. art. 139) had become the main proof of emancipation by the thirteenth century. The symbolical ceremonies that had come down from Frankish times—such as manumission in the churches on holy days—had pretty largely disappeared. Several chapters of the Bourgeois Assizes of Jerusalem-Cyprus contain interesting provisions concerning the enfranchisement of domestic slaves (xxvii, cciii–ccviii). Baptism of Saracen slaves was a frequent method of enfranchisement; they could not testify in court against their former master or any member of his family (xv–xvi).

[25] The Chronicle of Morea refers to the Frankish bishops as judges of the High Court, but adds that they could not take part in murder trials. (Greek Chronicle, ed. Schmitt, ll. 2013–16.)

[26] The *avoué* of an episcopal seigniory is called the *vidame.* The *avoué* and the *vidame* also represented their establishments in the secular lawsuits which these might have. The "golden age" of the *avoués* was the tenth cen-

Ecclesiastical justice proper, to which clerics were specially subject, is technically outside the scope of our discussion. But it calls for brief comment, especially since it also applied to laymen in a wide area of jurisdiction which we ordinarily think of as temporal. We may note first that it did not apply in a purely feudal case when the bishop or abbot who was also a feudatory was in contest with his suzerain or with another vassal. It succeeded to a remarkable degree in claiming jurisdiction over clerics who committed grave crimes, notably in England, where, after the unfortunate murder of archbishop Thomas Becket by royal courtiers, Henry II was forced to concede full "benefit of clergy."[27] The numerous causes for which church courts try laymen may be divided into (1) crimes against religion and morality, such as heresy, adultery, incest, divination, and attacks on churchmen; and (2) civil disputes relating to marriage, divorce, wills, tithes, breaches of oaths, the patronage of church benefices, etc. Archbishops and bishops often granted portions of this vast jurisdiction to abbots and even to laymen, on the model of grants of seignorial justice. The enlightened procedure and cheaper cost of ecclesiastical justice made it justly popular. But as the justice of the royal and important seignorial courts increased in efficiency, bitter jurisdictional conflicts broke out which reached their climax in the thirteenth century. The ecclesiastical judges were gradually limited to purely spiritual matters. Thus oaths were omitted from contracts, while the civil clauses of wills were regarded as their most essential portion, bringing them under the purview of secular courts.[28]

SEIGNORIAL FINANCE

An important baron or territorial ruler generally had the following sources of income. First, and easily most important, he lived off his own demesne, whose lands and population he exploited in a

tury and the first half of the eleventh. In Normandy the duke's protection of the monasteries made the *avoués* superfluous.

[27] The accused cleric could be tried only in a church court, which might degrade him and might even imprison him, but could not sentence him to death or maiming. Accused persons proved their clerical status simply by reading a passage from Scripture.

[28] Article 149 of the Assizes of Romania shows that jurisdiction over testamentary cases was not clearly defined in Morea. See also p. 156, above.

great variety of ways. Thus the actual cultivation of his lands was done by unpaid serfs, who also had to keep up the roads and seignior's buildings and perform military service without compensation. The lord levied a poll tax on his serfs and might tallage them arbitrarily. By the right known as the *banalités* he required his peasants to use his oven, his mill, and his winepress, and of course to pay for each use with a portion of the product.[1] From the free peasants the lord collected the payment called the *cens*, by which the peasants acknowledged the lord's superior rights of ownership in their land. He profited from commercial activity within his demesne, through customs and sales taxes and market rents. Finally, his profits from the administration of justice were a lucrative resource.

Secondly, as a feudal suzerain the lord enjoyed the income resulting from various obligations incumbent upon his vassals. We have described these obligations or rights elsewhere under the conventional heading of Aids and Incidents.[2]

Thirdly, a seignior whose lands included one or more bishoprics profited greatly from the right of *régale*, by which he took the income of the episcopal lands in the period—often deliberately prolonged—between the death of one bishop and the succession of another. Space permitting, many other methods might be cited to show how lay lords exploited church property, especially the lands of the monasteries, both before, and to a reduced extent after, the Cluniac and Gregorian reforms.[3]

The Assizes of Romania furnish several interesting details concerning the resources of the prince of Achaia. We have already indicated his rights over the servile population of his lands, as well as the aids and incidents to which he was entitled. He tended to reserve the control of ports and of salt-works (art. 84). He received the *cens* from free peasants (art. 192). He had well-recognized rights to treasure-trove (155). The revenues of his demesne lands were farmed out by the protovestiary (171). Similar rights and financial methods are to be found throughout the feudal world.

[1] See the summary of the condition of the Moreot serfs above, p. 173.
[2] Pages 127 ff., above.
[3] Cf. pp. 126 and 174, above.

Article 23 is of unusual interest for the definite manner in which it states that the prince must consult, and obtain the consent of, his vassals and subjects whenever he desires to raise money for public purposes by an extraordinary levy, other than the customary aids. This is a cogent statement of a fundamental feudal principle. It well stands comparison with chapters 12 and 14 of Magna Carta and is in fact wider in reference because the Charter safeguards the rights of the tenants-in-chief (and of London exceptionally) alone, while in Morea the "other freemen," such as the bourgeois, must agree to extraordinary exactions. Of course, no general doctrines of taxation or of parliamentary representation can be read into article 23, any more than into Magna Carta. McKechnie's words apply equally well to Morea: " 'No new exactions without consent of the individual taxed' was nearer the ideals of 1215 than 'no taxation without consent of Parliament.' Each 'baron' was summoned on his own behalf; and it is doubtful how far a dissenting minority could be bound by a decision of the rest." [4]

[4] W. S. McKechnie, *Magna Carta* (2d ed., Glasgow, 1914), p. 254. Cf. the interesting remarks of Sidney Painter, "Magna Carta," *American Historical Review*, October, 1947, pp. 42–49.

BIBLIOGRAPHY

EDITIONS OF THE TEXT

Les Assises de Romanie, edited by Georges Recoura, Paris, 1930; Bibliothèque de l'Ecole des Hautes Etudes, No. 258. This is the edition from which our translation was made. The text is in the old Venetian based on a manuscript of 1423. The French translation given by Recoura proved valuable on occasion though we have differed from him in a number of places. The Introduction to his edition is a masterpiece of textual and historical criticism.

Barbarorum leges antiquae, cum notis et glossariis, edited by Paolo Canciani, 5 vols., Venice, 1781–92. The text of the Assizes of Romania is in vol. III (1785), 493 ff. This is a less critical edition than that of Recoura, and little use was made of it in preparing our translation.

SOURCES OF FEUDAL LAW

1. IN THE EAST.

Asizai tou basileiou ton Hierosolymon kai tes Kyprou, kypriakoi nomoi, byzantina symbolaia, kretikai diathekai. Ed. K. Sathas, in Bibliotheca graeca medii aevi, vol. VI, Paris, 1877.

Assises d'Antioche. Reproduites en Français et publiées au sixième centenaire de la mort de Sempad le connétable, leur ancien traducteur arménien. Venice, 1876.

Assises de Jérusalem. Ed. Comte Beugnot. 2 vols., Paris, 1841–43. (Recueil des historiens des croisades: Lois, I–II.)

Assises du royaume de Jérusalem (textes français et italien); lre partie, Assises des Bourgeois, 2e partie, Le Plédéant et le Plaidoyer. Ed. Victor Foucher. 2 vols., Rennes, 1840.

Les Livres des Assises et des Usages deu reaume de Jérusalem. Ed. F. Kausler. Vol. I (no others published), Stuttgart, 1839.

2. IN THE WEST.

Bracton: *De Legibus et Consuetudinibus Angliae*. Ed. G. E. Woodbine. 4 vols., New Haven, Conn., 1915–41.

Coutumiers de Normandie. Ed. E. J. Tardif. Vol. I in 2 parts, Rouen, 1881, 1903; vol. II, Rouen, 1896.

De necessariis observantiis scaccarii dialogus; commonly called Dialogus de scaccario. By Richard, son of Nigel. Ed. A. Hughes, C. G. Crump, and C. Johnson. Oxford, 1902.

Las Siete Partidas, trans. into English by S. P. Scott, Chicago, 1931.

Les Établissements de Saint Louis. Ed. Paul Viollet. 4 vols., Paris, 1881–86.

Glanvill: *De Legibus et Consuetudinibus Regni Angliae*. Ed. G. E. Woodbine. New Haven, Conn., 1932. English translation by John Beames, Washington, D.C., 1900.

Philippe de Beaumanoir. *Coutumes de Beauvaisis*. Ed. A. Salmon. 2 vols., Paris, 1899–1900.

Des Sachsenspiegels erster und zweiter Theil. Ed. C. G. Homeyer. 2d ed., 3 vols., 1835–44. Erster Theil, 3d ed., 1861. Berlin.

Sachsenspiegel; land- und lehnrecht. Ed. K. A. Eckhardt. Hannover, 1933.

ENGLISH TRANSLATIONS OF DOCUMENTS ON FEUDALISM

The Glanvill and *Siete Partidas* cited above are the only translations of any major legal treatises. Shorter documents are to be found in:

Henderson, E.: *Select Historical Documents of the Middle Ages*, London, 1905. (Contains the Dialogue concerning the Exchequer, pp. 20–134.)

Stephenson, C. and Marcham, F. G.: *Sources of English Constitutional History*. N.Y. and London, 1937.

Thatcher, O. J. and McNeal, E. H.: *Source Book for Medieval History*. N.Y., 1905. (Feudalism, pp. 341–87.)

Translations and Reprints from the Original Sources of European History. Published by the Department of History of the University of Pennsylvania. Series I:

- vol. I, no. 6: *English Constitutional Documents*. (E. P. Cheyney)
- vol. II, no. 2: *Statistical Documents of the Middle Ages* (R. P. Falkner)
- vol. II, no. 5: *English Manorial Documents* (E. P. Cheyney)
- vol. IV, no. 3: *Documents Illustrative of Feudalism* (E. P. Cheyney)

vol. IV, no. 4: *Ordeals, Compurgation, Excommunication, Interdict* (A. P. Howland)
vol. VI, no. 5: *Laws of Charles the Great* (D. C. Munro)

SOURCES FOR THE HISTORY OF THE CRUSADER STATES OF GREECE

Acropolites, Georgius. *Opera*. Ed. A. Heisenberg. 2 vols., Leipsic, 1903.

Buchon, J. A. *Nouvelles recherches historiques sur la principauté française de Morée et ses hautes baronnies*. 2 vols., Paris, 1843.

Buchon, J. A. *Recherches et matériaux pour servir à une histoire de la domination française aux XIIIe, XIVe et XVe siècles dans les provinces démembrées de l'Empire grec à la suite de la quatrième croisade*. 2 vols., Paris, 1840.

Buchon, J. A. *Recherches historiques sur la principauté française de Morée et ses hautes baronnies*. 2 vols., Paris, 1845.

The Chronicle of Morea. To Chronikon tou Moreos. Greek text, ed. John Schmitt. London, 1904.

Chroniques gréco-romanes inédites ou peu connues. Ed. Charles Hopf. Berlin, 1873. (Contains Italian version of the Chronicle of Morea as well as Sanudo's Istoria del Regno di Romania.)

Libro de los Fechos et Conquistas del Principado de la Morea compilado por comandamiento de Don Fray Johan Ferrandez de Heredia maestro del Hospital de S. Johan de Jerusalem. Chronique de Morée aux XIIIe et XIVe siècles. Ed. Alfred Morel-Fatio. Geneva, 1885.

Livre de la conqueste de la princée de l'Amorée. Chronique de Morée (1204–1305). Ed. Jean Longnon. Paris, 1911.

To Chronikon tou Moreos. Ed. Petros P. Kalonaros. Athens, 1940. (An edition of the Greek version of the Chronicle of Morea with notes and critical apparatus in Modern Greek.)

Diplomatari de l'Orient Català (1301–1409). Ed. A. Rubió i Lluch. Barcelona, 1947.

Urkunden zur älteren Handels- und Staatsgeschichte der Republik Venedig. Ed. G. Tafel and G. M. Thomas. 3 vols., Vienna, 1856–57.

STUDIES IN THE FEUDAL INSTITUTIONS OF THE CRUSADER STATES

Christin, Pierre: *Étude des classes inférieures d'après les Assises de Jérusalem.* Poitiers, 1912.

Dodu, Gaston: *Histoire des institutions monarchiques dans le royaume latin de Jérusalem.* Paris, 1894.

Grandclaude, Maurice: "Liste d'assises remontant au premier royaume de Jérusalem (1099–1187)." *Mélanges Paul Fournier* (Paris 1929), 329–45.

Grandclaude, Maurice: *Étude critique sur les livres des Assises de Jérusalem.* Paris, 1923.

Hayek, Dimitri: *Le Droit franc en Syrie pendant les Croisades.* Paris, 1925.

La Monte, John L.: *Feudal Monarchy in the Latin Kingdom of Jerusalem, 1100–1291.* Cambridge, Mass., 1932.

LaMonte, John L.: "The Rise and Decline of a Frankish Seigneury in Syria in the Time of the Crusades," *Revue Historique du Sud-Est Européen,* (Bucharest) XV (1938), 301–22.

LaMonte, John L.: "Three Questions Concerning the Assises de Jérusalem," *Byzantina-Metabyzantina,* I, (1946), 201–11.

Meynial, Ed. "De quelques particularités des successions féodales dans les Assises de Jérusalem," *Revue nouvelle historique de droit français et étranger,* XVI (1892), 408–26.

Mitteis, Heinrich. "Ueber den liber consuetudinum Imperii Romaniae," in: *Studi di Storia e Diritto in onore di Enrico Besta.* Milan, 1939. II, pp. 68–97.

Preston, Helen: *Rural Conditions in the Kingdom of Jerusalem during the twelfth and thirteenth centuries.* Philadelphia, 1903.

Topping, Peter W.: "The Formation of the Assizes of Romania," *Byzantion,* XVII (1944–45), 304–14.

SECONDARY WORKS ON THE HISTORY OF THE CRUSADER STATES

Atiya, A. S. *The Crusade in the Later Middle Ages.* London, 1938

Buchon, J. A. *Histoire des conquêtes et de l'établissement des Français dans les états de l'ancienne Grèce sous les Ville-Hardoin, à la suite de la quatrième croisade.* Vol. I (no others published), Paris, 1846.

Buchon, J. A. *Voyage dans l'Eubée, les îles ionniennes et les Cy-*

clades en 1841. Ed. Jean Longnon, with "Notice biographique et bibliographique." Paris, 1911.

Cahen, Claude. *La Syrie du Nord à l'époque des croisades et la principauté franque d'Antioche*. Paris, 1940.

Cerone, Francesco. *La sovranità napoletana sulla Morea e sulle isole vicine*. Archivio storico per le province napoletane, vol. XLI (Naples, 1916), pp. 5–64, 193–266; vol. XLII (1917), pp. 5–67.

Chapman, Conrad. *Michel Paléologue*. Paris, 1926.

Dragoumis, S. N. *Chronikon Moreos: toponymika, topographika, historika*. Athens, 1921. (In Modern Greek.)

DuCange, Charles DuFresne. *Histoire de l'empire de Constantinople sous les empereurs français jusqu'à la conquête des Turcs*. 2 vols. Ed. J. A. Buchon, Paris, 1826.

Fotheringham, J. K. *Marco Sanudo, Conqueror of the Archipelago*. Oxford, 1915.

Gerland, Ernst. *Geschichte des lateinischen Kaiserreiches von Konstantinopel*. I. Teil: *Geschichte der Kaiser Balduin I. und Heinrich 1204–1216*. Homburg v. d. Höhe, 1905.

Gregorovius, F. A. *Geschichte der Stadt Athen im Mittelalter*. 2 vols., Stuttgart, 1889. (Modern Greek translation and edition by S. P. Lampros in 3 vols., the third consisting of new documents, Athens, 1904–06.)

Heyd, Wilhelm von. *Histoire du commerce du Levant au moyen-âge*. Trans. by Furcy Raynaud. 2 vols., Leipsic, 1885–86. Réimpression, 1923.

Hopf, Carl. *Geschichte Griechenlands vom Beginn des Mittelalters bis auf unsere Zeit*. 2 vols., Leipsic, 1867–68. Published as part of the article "Griechenland" in Ersch and Gruber, Allgemeine Encyclopädie der Wissenschaften und Künste, vols. 85 and 86.

Iorga, N. *France de Constantinople et de Morée*. Bucarest, 1935.

Longnon, Jean. *Les Français d'outre-mer au moyen-âge. Essai sur l'expansion française dans le bassin de la Méditerranée*. Paris, 1929.

Longnon, Jean. "Problèmes de l'histoire de la principauté de Morée," *Journal des Savants*, April–June 1946, 77–93, and July–December 1946, 147–61.

Longnon, Jean. "Le Rattachement de la principauté de Morée au royaume de Sicile en 1267," *Journal des Savants*, July–December 1942, 134–43.

Longnon, Jean. *Recherches sur la vie de Geoffroy de Villehardouin suivies du catalogue des actes des Villehardouin.* Paris, 1939.

Meyer, Ernst. *Peloponnesische wanderungen; reisen und forschungen zur antiken und mittelalterlichen topographie von Arkadien und Achaia.* Zürich and Leipsic, 1939.

Miller, William. *Essays on the Latin Orient.* Cambridge, Eng., 1921.

Miller, William, "Greece and the Aegean under Frank and Venetian Domination (1204–1571)." Chap. XV in *Cambridge Medieval History,* vol. IV, New York, 1923, pp. 432–77.

Miller, William. *The Latins in the Levant. A History of Frankish Greece (1204–1566).* London, 1908. (Enlarged translation in Modern Greek by S. P. Lampros, 2 vols., Athens, 1909–10.)

Rey, E. G. *Les colonies franques en Syrie aux XIIme et XIIIme siècles.* Paris, 1883.

Rodd, Sir James Rennell. *The Princes of Achaia and the Chronicles of Morea. A Study of Greece in the Middle Ages.* 2 vols., London, 1907.

Zakythinos, D. A. *Le Despotat grec de Morée.* Tome premier: Histoire politique. Paris, 1932.

SECONDARY WORKS ON FEUDAL INSTITUTIONS

Adams, G. B. *Constitutional History of England.* Rev. by R. L. Schuyler. New York, 1936.

Adams, G. B. *Council and Courts in Anglo-Norman England.* New Haven, 1926.

Adams, G. B. *The Origin of the English Constitution.* New Haven, 1912.

Barraclough, Geoffrey, tr. and ed. *Mediaeval Germany, 911–1250.* 2 vols., Oxford, 1938. Vol. II.

Bloch, Marc. *Les caractères originaux de l'histoire rurale française.* Oslo, 1931.

Bloch, Marc. *La Société féodale. I La Formation des liens de dépendance.* Paris, 1939.

Bloch, Marc. *La Société féodale. II Les Classes et le gouvernement des hommes.* Paris, 1940.

Brissaud, Jean. *A History of French Private Law.* Tr. by R. Howell. Boston, 1912.

Brissaud, Jean. *A History of French Public Law.* Tr. by J. W. Garner. Boston, 1915.

Brunner, Heinrich. *Deutsche Rechtsgeschichte.* 2 vols., Leipsic,

1887–92. 2d ed., vol. I, 1906; vol. II, 1928, by Claudius von Schwerin.

Brunner, Heinrich. *Forschungen zur Geschichte des deutschen und französischen Rechtes.* Stuttgart, 1894.

Brussel, Nicolas. *Nouvel examen de l'usage général des fiefs en France, pendant les onzième, douzième, treizième et quatorzième siècles.* 2 vols., Paris, 1750.

Cahen, Claude. *Le Régime féodal de l'Italie normande.* Paris, 1940.

Calmette, J. *La Société féodale.* 4th ed., Paris, 1938.

Carlyle, R. W. and A. J. *A History of Mediaeval Political Theory in the West.* Vol. III (by A. J. Carlyle). Edinburgh and London, 1928.

Coulton, G. G. *The Medieval Village.* Cambridge, Eng., 1926.

Didier, N. *Le droit des fiefs dans la coutume de Hainaut au moyen âge.* Paris, 1945.

Esmein, A. *Cours élémentaire d'histoire du droit français.* 14th ed., by R. Génestal, Paris, 1921.

Ganshof, F.-L. "Contribution à l'étude des origines des cours féodales en France," *Revue historique de droit français et étranger*, 1928. (Reprint, 22 p.)

Ganshof, F.-L. Étude sur l'administration de la justice dans la région bourguignonne de la fin du Xe au début du XIIIe siècle," *Revue historique,* CXXXV (Sept.–Dec. 1920), 193–218.

Ganshof, F.-L. "La juridiction du seigneur sur son vassal à l'époque carolingienne," *Revue de l'Université de Bruxelles,* Nos. 9–10, June–July, 1922. (Reprint, 12 p.)

Ganshof, F.-L. "Note sur la compétence des cours féodales en France," in *Mélanges d'histoire offerts à Henri Pirenne,* 2 vols., Brussels, 1926, I, 161–70.

Ganshof, F.-L. *Qu'est-ce que la féodalité?* Brussels, 1944. 2nd ed., Brussels and Neuchâtel, 1947.

Gleason, S. E. *An Ecclesiastical Barony of the Middle Ages: the Bishopric of Bayeux 1066–1204.* Cambridge, Mass., 1936.

Guilhiermoz, P. *Essai sur l'origine de la noblesse en France au moyen âge.* Paris, 1902.

Halphen, L. "Les institutions judiciaires en France au XIe siècle. Région angévine," *Revue historique,* LXXVII (Sept.–Dec. 1901), 279–307.

Haskins, C .H. *Norman Institutions.* Cambridge, Mass., 1918.

Huebner, Rudolf. *A History of Germanic Private Law.* Trans. by

F. S. Philbrick. Boston, 1918. (Continental Legal History Series.)

Lea, H. C. *Superstition and Force.* 4th ed., Philadelphia, 1892.

Luchaire, Achille. *Manuel des institutions françaises.* Paris, 1892.

McIlwain, C. H. *The Growth of Political Thought in the West.* New York, 1932.

McKechnie, W. S. *Magna Carta. A Commentary on the Great Charter of King John.* 2d ed., Glasgow, 1914.

Mitteis, Heinrich. *Lehnrecht und Staatsgewalt.* Weimar, 1933.

Odegaard, Charles E. *Vassi and Fideles in the Carolingian Empire.* Cambridge, Mass., 1945.

Painter, S. *French Chivalry. Chivalric Ideas and Practices in Mediaeval France.* Baltimore, 1940.

Painter, S. "Magna Carta," *American Historical Review,* LIII (1947–48), 42–49.

Pollock, Sir F., and Maitland, F. W. *The History of English Law before the Time of Edward I.* 2d ed., Cambridge, Eng., 2 vols., 1898.

Sczaniecki, Michel. *Essai sur les fiefs-rentes.* Paris, 1946.

Stenton, F. M. *The First Century of English Feudalism, 1066–1166.* Oxford, 1932.

Stephenson, Carl. *Mediaeval Feudalism.* Ithaca, N.Y., 1942.

Stephenson, Carl. "The Origin and Significance of Feudalism." *American Historical Review.* XLVI (1940–41), pp. 788–812.

Thompson, J. W. *Feudal Germany.* Chicago, 1928.

Vasiliev, A. A. "On the Question of Byzantine Feudalism." *Byzantion,* VIII (1933), pp. 584–604.

Vernadsky, George. "Feudalism in Russia." *Speculum,* XIV (1939), pp. 300–23.

INDEX

(The italicized figures in square brackets refer to the numbered articles or chapters of the Assizes of Romania. The figures in roman type, not enclosed, refer to pages of the Introduction, Commentary, or Prologue of the Assizes.)